𝔚𝔞𝔫𝔡𝔢𝔯𝔩𝔲𝔰𝔱

Travel off the Tourist Track

David J. Patten

David J. Patten

Pattented Press, Saint Petersburg, FL

ISBN: 13:978-1978209411
ISBN: 10:197820941X
Library of Congress Control Number: 2017916401
Create Space Independent Publishing Platform,
    North Charleston, SC

On the cover:
Planet Earth as seen from outer space

Foreword

Wanderlust: a strong impulse or desire to wander, travel about, and to see the world.

From the German: "wander" and "desire"

"The term originates from the German words *wandern* (to hike) and *lust* (desire). The term *wandern*, frequently misused as a false friend, does in fact not mean "to wander", but "to hike." Placing the two words together, translated: "enjoyment of hiking", although it is commonly described as an enjoyment of strolling, roaming about or wandering.

"In modern German, the use of the word *wanderlust* to mean "desire to travel" is less common, having been replaced by *fernweh* (literally, "farsickness"), coined as an antonym to *heimweh* ("homesickness")."

From: https://en.wikipedia.org/wiki/Wanderlust

Wanderlust is a book for those with an addiction to travel. It is for experienced travelers and adventurers eager to travel well off the beaten tourist track. **Wanderlust** is for those who become inspired when serendipitously finding sites off in remote and little-known places. It is for those who are eager to explore sites discovered while on a trip in depth and not just with the attitude of having been there and done that.

These articles explore in detail various sites visited during the last fourteen years of travel since retirement. Travel requires having the necessary time, health, stamina and financial resources, so I feel especially fortunate to have had all four.

In order to cover more exotic destinations, North America and Europe have been excluded in this book. On the other hand, most other major regions of the world have been covered by including sites in Central and South America, Africa, the Caucasus, the Near East, South Asia, Southeast Asia, the Far East, and Oceania.

These articles follow a set format, first giving the official country name, site name, location and the date the site was visited. Information on UNESCO World Heritage Site status is given where appropriate. At the end of each article, websites that were consulted when conducting the research for the articles are cited that can also be referred to for additional information.

Regrettably, in order to keep down this book's publication costs, only very limited numbers of photographs could be included. If readers wish to view more photographs of the sites covered in this volume, they are strongly encouraged to consult the websites cited at the ends of the various articles.

I must admit to relying heavily on information from the internet, and especially from the *Wikipedia*, for the articles in this book. Guidebooks such as the *DK Eyewitness Guides* and the *Lonely Planet* series often give very little information, if any, on the off-the-tourist-track sites included here. They also usually include much more information on accommodations and places to eat than on the sites to be visited at travel destinations. Information on the internet was also often found to be more up-to-date than that found in guidebooks, many of which were written years ago.

The *Wikipedia* and UNESCO websites have usually been preferred over other websites. While the *Wikipedia* has been criticized as lacking in accuracy, experience has shown that its entries are often much more factually balanced than other websites consulted. *Wikipedia* entries have been edited, and unsubstantiated statements are often marked with the note, "citation needed." Information on such websites as *TripAdvisor* usually tends to be essentially the unsubstantiated opinions of travelers.

Since a second, revised, and expanded edition of this book may be published, readers are invited to report any misinformation or inaccuracies in these articles to the author at: djpatten@tampabay.rr.com.

Hours of opening, admission fees, on-site information in English, etc. are very subject to change, so such information has not been given in the articles. It is assumed that experienced travelers will be able to locate and verify such information on their own.

Before embarking on the publication of these articles, most of my writing on travel has been published in *International Travel News (ITN)*. Starting in 2009, *ITN* has published twenty-three such articles. Most have been short articles with two being feature articles, one of them a cover story.

Thirteen of the articles in this collection were originally published in *International Travel News*, but most have been extensively revised and enlarged. David Tykol, editor of *ITN* assures me that republication of the articles first published in *ITN* is permitted. As stated by *ITN*: "All materials submitted become the property of *ITN*, which has explicit reprint rights. However, authors still retain all rights."

The thirteen articles originally published in *ITN* are as follows:

I hope your interest will be captivated, as mine was, by the sites covered in these articles and that you will become inspired to visit some of them yourself, if you haven't already. Better yet would be for you to form your own list of favorite off-the-tourist-track sites.

Travel has been for me a life-transforming experiencem and Mark Twain has already said it much better than I ever could:

"Travel is fatal to prejudice, bigotry, and narrow-mindedness, and many of our people need it sorely on these accounts. Broad, wholesome, charitable views of men and things cannot be acquired by vegetating in one little corner of the earth all one's lifetime."

In conclusion, I also quote Rick Steves who always says at the end of his TV programs, "Keep on traveling."

David J. Patten

Saint Petersburg, FL

Acknowledgments

My most faithful e-mail correspondent has requested that he remain anonymous, but he has undoubtedly been of the greatest assistance in the writing of this book. He has proofread every one of the thirty-six articles and has always responded quickly with corrections and comments. This book would not have been possible without his unfailing support.

Ralph Hamblin, graphic artist, published writer, and former colleague, at the *Saint Petersburg Times* (now the *Tampa Bay Times*) is also to be thanked for his feedback and his many constructive criticisms.

As very much a world traveler, Jill Athey, must be acknowledged for her support and advice. She has been such a great source of inspiration and a most congenial travel companion on all seven trips we have taken together as singles.

Professor Francis B. Randall of Sarah Lawrence College, Bronxville, N.Y. must be acknowledged for his broad background in ancient history and for his feedback on such articles as that on Hippo Regius, Algeria, and the libraries, ancient and modern, of Alexandria, Egypt.

Elaine Svenonius, Professor Emerita, Department of Information Studies, UCLA, is also to be acknowledged for her advice on the article on the libraries of Alexandria, Egypt.

Judith Schrafft, published travel writer, has also done much to inspire my own writing on travel and is to be thanked for her meticulous proofreading and editing skills.

David Tykol, Editor, *International Travel News (ITN)*, must be cited for his many constructive, critical comments and his editing of the articles published in ITN.

Also, Beth Habian, Features Editor, *ITN*, must be mentioned for her outstanding work in the editing of the two feature articles published in *ITN* and for her selection of one of my photographs for the cover of *ITN*'s April 2016 issue.

David J. Patten
Saint Petersburg, FL

About the Author

The author photographed at the Jantar Mantar, Jaipur, India, in May 2004

David J. Patten is a travel writer, travel photographer, graphic designer, and world traveler, based in Saint Petersburg, Florida.

Patten graduated *summa cum laude* with an undergraduate degree in art from the University of Nebraska, Omaha. He has a master's degree in art history from the State University of Iowa, Iowa City, and a master's degree in information science from the University of Michigan, Ann Arbor.

He has held staff positions at the University of Cincinnati, Washington University, St. Louis, and Oberlin College, Ohio. He worked for ten years as the editor of an art periodicals indexing service at a New York City publishing firm. He also held the position of index editor at an art indexing and abstracting service of the J. Paul Getty Trust based in Williamstown, Massachusetts.

Before retiring, he held the position of graphic designer at the *Saint Petersburg Times*, now *The Tampa Bay Times*.

He has traveled to a total of fifty-six countries with forty-eight of them having been visited since retiring in 2003. While living in New York City, his travels, primarily in Europe, included visiting an additional eight countries.

His writing on travel includes twenty-three articles published in *International Travel News (ITN)*. His travel photographs have been published in *International Travel News* and the *Saint Petersburg Times* and exhibited at the Morean Arts Center, Saint Petersburg, Florida.

His most recent publication is an anthology of seven science fiction short stories, *Skyscape Scans*, available on Amazon.

He invites readers to contact him at: djpatten@tampabay.rr.com.

Table of Contents

Table of Contents (continued)

Countries Covered by World Regions

Central America & the Caribbean
    Cuba, Guatemala, Mexico
South America
    Peru, Chile
Africa
    Algeria, Egypt, Ethiopia, Morocco, Tunisia
Middle East
    Iran, Israel, Jordan, Turkey
The Caucasus
    Armenia, Azerbaijan, Georgia
South Asia
    India, Sri Lanka
Central Asia
    Kazakhstan, Uzbekistan
Southeast Asia
    Cambodia, Indonesia, Laos, Myanmar, Thailand, Vietnam
Far East
    China, Japan, Korea, Taiwan
Oceania
    Rapa Nui (Easter Island) - Annexed by Chile

ALGERIA

Country name: People's Democratic Republic of **Algeria**

Site name: Hippo Regius

Location: On the Mediterranean coast, near present-day Annaba

Date of Visit: 2 October 2014

Saint Augustine of Hippo Regius

Hippo Regius is, in my estimation, one of North Africa's most important, ruined, Roman cities. Because of its resident bishop, Saint Augustine, its role within the development of Western Christianity has been profound. It therefore seems most unfortunate that it has not been designated a UNESCO World Heritage Site as Algeria's Djémila, Timgad and Tipasa have been.

Hippo Regius, located on the river Ubus and near the present-day city of Annaba, has also been called Hippona. When taken by the French in 1832 it was renamed Bone or Bona and made a governmental center in the department of Algeria. It appears that Hippo acquired the designation, "Regius," meaning

"of the king," back at a time when it was the residence of Numidian kings   .

Today Hippo Regius appears even more neglected by the Algerians than do so many of its other ancient Roman cities. The excavations at Hippo are said to have been made primarily by Erwan Marec, a French naval officer. Little appears to have been done at the site in the last fifty years since then. It also appears to be among the least visited of Algeria's ancient sites in that we had the ancient city almost totally to ourselves except for local guards and our police escort that accompanied us almost the entire time we were in Algeria. Nevertheless, the site looks to be well kept and evidences little damage from tourism.

Near the site's entrance is a residential section, with the Villa of the Labyrinth and Villa of the Procurateur being the most impressive. The city also has what is said to be one of North Africa's largest Roman forums. It also had a notable sewer system in that while touring the city I was informed by our guide that I was walking over a paved sewer line imbedded in one of its streets.

What I found to be the most interesting was the so-called Christian quarter with its baptistry and large, Christian basilica. The outlines of the basilica, unusual in that it faced north rather than east, is quite obvious in the existing ruins. The nave measures an impressive 37m by 18.5m with its length being twice its width. Remnants of bases of columns define what were once side aisles. The basilica's apse appears even more clearly defined by the bench that survives, outlining its semi-circular form. As I surveyed the ancient basilica, I wondered if Hippo's most famous resident, Saint Augustine, might have seated himself on the existing bench of the ancient structure's apse.

After an early life as somewhat of a libertine, Saint Augustine is said to have retired to what he hoped would be a life of peaceful contemplation in North Africa. It was at Hippo that he was destined to produce his two most famous works, his *Confessions* (Latin: *Confessiones*) and the *The City of God Against the Pagans* (Latin: *De ciuitate Dei contra paganos*), most often called *The City of God*. Both were to prove later to exert profound influence on the evolution of Christianity in the Western world. Living for seventy-five years from 354 CE until his death on 28 August 430 CE, Saint Augustine is known to have been one of seven bishops of Hippo.

It is largely because of Saint Augustine that today Hippo remains the location of a hospital of the Little Sisters of the Poor and of the magnificent Basilica de Saint Augustine built by the French in 1881 that sits on a hill overlooking the ancient ruins of the city. The site is also said to be the location of a small museum in what had previously been a penitentiary, a part of the site that we missed seeing.

On the other hand, we found it to be possible to visit the Basilica de Saint Augustine, a 19th century creation attempting to combine Western style architectural elements with more Near Eastern ones, especially on its exterior. The basilica appeared to be exceptionally well kept by Augustinian priests, and the archbishop of Algiers has said that his jurisdiction numbers some 10,000 Catholics.

The large church was found to have many chapels, stained glass windows and well preserved, colorful, painted decoration. Most impressive was the effigy of Saint Augustine, encased in a glass coffin, behind the main altar. A relic of the saint, his elbow from his right arm, is said to have been placed in the appropriate position inside the effigy. The remainder of the saint's remains were first moved to Sardinia and then to Pavia, Italy, where they remain to this day.

Hippo's importance in the evolution of Western Christianity resides not only in being the city where Saint Augustine served as bishop. It is also notable for hosting numerous church councils and synods. Church councils are known to have taken place at Hippo in 383, 394, and 426 CE. It was at the Synod at Hippo in 393 CE and the Synod at Carthage in 397 CE that a list of the books now in the Bible's New Testament was compiled. It seems especially interesting that the list survives as the basis for the Douay Bible's scriptures and contains a number of books regarded as apocryphal by Protestantism.

Little did I realize that I would find an ancient site in Algeria notable as the location where two of the most influential Western Christianity's theological texts were written by such an renowned theologian as the Early Christian patriarch, Saint Augustine.

Adapted from:

http://en.wikipedia.org/wiki/Hippo_Regius

https://www.mosaicnorthafrica.com/portfolio/hippo-regius/

http://faculty.georgetown.edu/jod/algeria/algeria-sitevisits.html

ARMENIA

Country: Republic of Armenia

Site: Garni, Kotayk province, southeast of Yerevan

Location: Garni Historical and Cultural Museum Reserve, 32 km. southeast of Armenia's capital of Yerevan.

Date Visited: 18 September 2011

Armenia's Pagan Temple at Garni

Finding such a beautifully restored, Hellenistic style, pagan temple in a country so well known for its early Christian architecture came as a great surprise.

Armenia is credited with being the first nation to recognize Christianity as the state religion. It was St. Gregory the Illuminator who converted King Tiridates III to Christianity in 301 CE. Declared the first Catholicos of the Armenian Apostolic Church, it was St. Gregory who proceeded to demolish many pagan shrines and temples and who constructed many churches and monasteries in their place.

Located on a spectacular site overlooking the Azat River, a first century palace complex was built that included fortified walls, soldiers' and servants' quarters, a summer palace, a temple and a later 3rd-4th century Roman bath. Today, the beautifully reconstructed temple sits on a triangular site that juts over the river gorge by 10 meters while the fourth side was guarded by a fortified wall 180 meters in length.

According to Pliny the Elder, it was in the 1st century CE that the Arshakuni King T'rdat I introduced the Roman emperor, Nero, to certain magical rites. At the same time the cult of Mithra was added to the Roman pantheon. After giving homage to Nero in Rome, King T'rdat is credited as having received 2 million *sesterces* from Nero to rebuild his capital which the king named Neroneia in Nero's honor. At about the same time, T'rdat commissioned the temple at Garni.

Further evidence of the 1st century date for Garni's pagan temple is located on the founding stone discovered at the site which was later carved into a *khachkar*, or stone memorial cross. Unknown for centuries, the Greek inscription was discovered by archaeologists who, rolling over the large stone, found the inscription giving a 1st century date rather than the 2nd century CE date given earlier to the site.

Although there are other important ancient remains at Garni, it is the beautifully restored temple that is Garni's main attraction. Sitting high on an elevated platform, it is a peripteros, Greco-Roman temple. The exterior is surrounded by 24 Ionic columns. Constructed of basalt, the temple is unlike the many other Hellenistic examples built from softer stone. Its exact date of construction is in some dispute with the temple reputedly having been built either in 115 CE or in 175 CE.

Built as a declaration of Armenia as a Roman province, some say the temple may have housed a statue of the emperor Trajan. Others contend that it may have been built as a tomb for the Armeno-Roman ruler, Sohaemus.

There are also indications that it may have been dedicated to the Zoroastrian-influenced, Armenian, mythological solar deity, Mihr, often considered the equivalent of Mithra.

When Armenia became Christian, the temple was used as a summer house for Armenian royalty. After being destroyed by an earthquake in 1679, the site remained in ruins until the reconstruction was undertaken between 1969 and 1975.

Visiting Garni and seeing one of Armenia's architectural gems, especially one honoring a pagan deity, was one of the highlights of the trip to Armenia in September of 2011.

It is especially ironic that it is not the early Christian architecture of Armenia that has had the most profound influences on Western architecture. It is the pagan, Greco-Roman architecture such as that found at Garni that has influenced so much of the architecture of the Western world. Whenever you see a portico with classically fluted columns supporting a gabled pediment, you are seeing the influence of ancient Greco-Roman architecture such as seen at Christian Armenia's pagan temple at Garni.

Adapted from:
https://en.wikipedia.org/wiki/Temple_of_Garni
http://www.atb.am/en/armenia/sights/christ/garni/
http://www.advantour.com/armenia/garni.htm

AZERBAIJAN

Country name: Republic of Azerbaijan

Site name: Summer Palace of the Sheki Khans

Location: Sheki, in northern Azerbaijan, 325 km (202 miles) from Baku

UNESCO World Heritage Site: Tentative listing for the city of Sheki, no. 1576, Summited 24 October 2001; the Summer Palace was nominated as a UNESCO site, 1998

Date of Visit: 24 September 2011

An Ornate Summer Palace: Azerbaijan's Palace of the Skeki Khans

Horror vacui is a Latin term meaning "fear of empty space," also called "kenophobia." It is often cited as a characteristic of Asian art and is intended to describe the filling of every possible surface or space with some form of detail or decoration.

The extreme richness of the lavish decoration of the Summer Palace at Sheki, Azerbaijan, is, I feel, an ideal example of such attention to ornamental detail.

Built from 1761 to 1762 as the summer palace of Hussein-khan Mushtad, the grandson of Gadzhi Chelebi, the summer palace is the only extant portion of the palatial fortress of the Sheki Khans of northern Azerbaijan. Originally, the fortress contained a winter palace, residences for the Kahns' families, and quarters for servants. Today, only the summer palace remains. Also, only two plane trees remain of what originally were extensive gardens with pools and trees.

The building, constructed of brick, river rock and wood from plane and oak trees, is a rectangular, two-story structure covered by a hip, wooden roof with broad eaves. It measures 32m by 8.5m on its exterior. The layout of rooms is the same on both of the building's levels. Three rooms are arranged side-by-side in a row and are separated by narrow *iwans* that serve to give access to the rooms. Two stairways on the building's north provide access to the palace's second floor. Access to the floors is separated into the public and private sections of the floors. The first floor was primarily for use by the public and clerks; the second, for the family of the Khans and their guests.

The lavishly decorated façade of the palace is one of the first aspects of the palace that attracted our attention. Decorative tile work in blue, turquoise and ochre as well as painted panels with floral motifs decorate much of the façade. On the lower level, the *iwans* are outlined with gold, while on the upper story, niches are decorated with mirrored *muqarnas*. Especially prominent on the façade are the windows with their latticework of wood and that have been constructed without adhesives or nails. Filling the spaces created by the latticework are multi-colored glass mosaics. It has been estimated that up to 5,000 pieces of small panes of colored glass per square meter have been used to create the stained glass windows.

The palace's interior is another showpiece of decorative detail. The windows and doorways have been artfully constructed of small sections of wood and colored Venetian glass, so the interiors are lighted with such rainbow hues as reds, blues, greens and yellows. Each interior room is decorated somewhat differently with walls and ceilings frescoed with miniature paintings, birds, flowers, gardens and various animals.

Intended for access by the public, the first floor's interiors have been decorated to display the power and wealth of the Khans. Trees, flowers, and animals have been used as symbols of fertility. The palace's second floor is divided into two sections; one section for women, the other for men. The section for women has been decorated with oriental motifs and flowers. The section for men is considered the most richly decorated of the interior spaces. It was intended to display the military power of the Khans and features military attire, banners and various weapons. Hunting scenes cover some walls, while the ceilings display the Khans' coat of arms and other symbols of authority.

Since its construction in the 18th century, the palace has undergone numerous restorations. Restorations from 1955 to 1965 were undertaken by Nivazi Rzaev and architects Kamal Mamedbekov and Nikolai Utsyn. The most recent restoration was performed from 2002 to 2004 by a team of German restorers from the firm, Neumühler Bauhütte GmbH.

The city of Sheki has been tentatively listed on the UNESCO World Heritage Sites list, while the summer palace has been nominated for the list in 1998 by the president of the Azerbaijan Committee of the International Council on Monuments and Sites (ICOMOS).

Due to delays created by our entry into Azerbaijan from Georgia, we arrived in Sheki after the palace was due to close. We felt especially grateful that officials in charge of the palace kept it open past the closing time just so we could see not only its elegantly decorated exterior but also see its very lavishly decorated interior.

While our guide in Georgia was among the poorest during our trip to the Caucasus, we were grateful that our guides in Azerbaijan were among the very best, especially our exceptionally vivacious guide in Azerbaijan's capital city of Baku.

Adapted from:

https://en.wikipedia.org/wiki/Palace_of_Shaki_Khans

http://www.discoverazerbaijan.az/discover/discover-azerbaijan/sheki-khans-palace/

http://www.advantour.com/azerbaijan/sheki/sheki-khan-castle.htm

http://whc.unesco.org/en/tentativelists/1576/

CAMBODIA

Country name: Kingdom of Cambodia

Site name: Leper King Terrace

Location: Angkor Thom, Angkor

UNESCO World Heritage Site: no. 668, inscribed 1992

Date of Visit : 14 December 2009

Secrets of Angkor's Leper King Terrace

Most tours to Cambodia's ancient Khmer capital of Angkor include a stop at the Elephant Terrace. You might also be allowed to take a look at the so called Leper King Terrace located north and to your right as you face the Elephant Terrace. Both terraces are located in the northwest corner of Angkor Thom's Royal Square.

Only if you have one of Cambodia's best guides will there be a mention of the narrow corridor excavated behind the façade of the Leper King Terrace. It can only be entered along the side of the terrace to your left as you face the terrace. If you have the time to visit the corridor cut in the terrace, you will be rewarded by seeing ancient wall reliefs hidden for centuries inside the terrace. They are among some of Angkor's finest and best preserved examples of Khmer art.

Unfortunately, the name of the terrace is a misnomer. Dating from the late 12th century CE and built in Angkor's Bayon style under Javavarman VII, the terrace has been incorrectly named because of the 15th century image sitting atop it. Also, the nude, kneeling figure, once discolored by white spots of lichen, has probably been misidentified as representing King Yasovarman I, reputed as having had leprosy according to an ancient legend. Most archaeologists now believe the figure represents Yama, the Hindu deity of the underworld and death.

Also, the statue presently located at the terrace in Angkor is only a replica of the original. The original figure resides under its own canopy in the center of the courtyard of the National Museum in Phnom Penh. Although only a copy, repairs to the figure's neck evidence that the head is a replacement. Thieves succeeded in even stealing the original head of the replica.

The nudity of the figure is quite unusual in Khmer art, and the figure's kneeling pose has been thought to reflect Javanese influence. The image is also thought to have originally been holding an object, but what it might have been is unknown.

Controversy still centers around the terrace's function. Some believe it was used for royal festivals. Others believe it was used as a royal cremation site.

Still more controversy surrounds the reason for the construction of the two façades of the terrace with the earlier reliefs being covered over by later ones. Perhaps a larger terrace was needed, or perhaps the original façade proved to be structurally unstable. The present outer façade, which has reliefs similar to those of the inner wall, appears to have been built to extend the size of the terrace, while rubble filled in the space between the two walls.

Due to excavations in the 1990s by the École Française d'Extrême-oriente (EFEO), the inner wall's magnificently preserved reliefs can now be viewed by entering the long, narrow corridor formed by high walls some six meters in height on either side.

Since similar subjects decorate both inner and outer walls, the second wall and its reliefs are thought not to have been intended as being an improvement over the original carvings. The rough chisel marks on some of the images on the inner walls have also caused some scholars to believe it was never finished.

Subjects of the reliefs include deities of the underworld, heavenly women called *apsaras*, kings, warriors carrying swords, sea creatures, and multi-headed serpents or *nagas*. Notable on the outer wall are an image of Shiva holding a trident and a representation of a sword swallower.

Since the carvings on the outer terrace wall show many signs of weathering, visiting the corridor and its inner wall allowed me to see some of Angkor's best preserved relief carvings. I was able to appreciate even more fully the truly magnificent artistic achievements of the ancient sculptors who carved such masterworks of Khmer sculpture.

Adapted from:

https://en.wikipedia.org/wiki/Terrace_of_the_Leper_King

https://www.renown-travel.com/cambodia/angkor/royalterraces.html

http://www.tourismcambodia.com/attractions/angkor/terrace-of-leper-king.htm

CHILE

Country name: Republic of Chile (Spanish: República de Chile)

Site name: Museo de Arqueología e Historia Francisco Fonck

Location: Viña del Mar, Chile

Tour Dates: 2-9 January 2009

Easter Island Artifacts in Chile: Museo Fonck

The primary reason for the visit to Chile was ultimately to visit Rapa Nui, also known as Easter Island. In 2009, Easter Island was accessible via LAN Airlines only from Santiago, Chile. Since then, I understand there are flights from Lima, Peru.

Although it was listed on my itinerary, I never did get inside the small museum located on Easter Island. On my last day on the island, I finally found the island's only museum located far outside the island's town of Hanga Roa. Even then, I only had the time to photograph the museum's exterior and several of the large, modern sculptures made by the islanders located on the museum's grounds.

Named after a German priest, Sebastián Englert, the small museum, that includes a nearby library, contains about 15,000 artifacts, primarily stone implements. Unfortunately, the museum's Rongo Rongo tablets containing the islanders' ancient writing are only copies. Of the twenty-seven known tablets to have survived, none remain on the island but survive only in museums around the world.

Since Rapa Nui had been annexed by Chile in 1888, I found that two small museums on mainland Chile had collections of artifacts from the island.

On my own, I finally found the small museum tucked away to one side of the the Basilico de la Merced in central Santiago. In spite of having only one small gallery devoted to Easter Island, the artifacts were among some of the finest I'd seen anywhere. I would only rate the the one small showcase in the Metropolitan Museum of Art in New York City as displaying a comparable collection. Only in the museum of La Merced, did I find it possible to see an original Rongo Rongo tablet containing the mysterious writing of the ancient islanders which has yet to be deciphered.

Knowing my interest in Rapa Nui artifacts, my local Chilean guide was kind enough to make a point of taking me to the Museo Arqueología e Historia Francisco Fonck located in Viña del Mar, outside Valparaíso. In 1937 the ethnographical and archaeological museum was founded primarily to focus on Chile's history. Then in 1985 the home of the wealthy Délano family of Viña del Mar was acquired by the local municipal authorities to be used to house the museum. The museum was named after the German doctor and pioneer archaeologist, Franz Adolf Fonck Foveaux (1830-1912), but better known as Francisco Fonck.

At the time of my visit, there was a special exhibition of shrunken heads being promoted by the museum. Since time for visiting the museum was very limited, I missed seeing anything on the museum's second floor, so I missed such exhibits as a collection of stuffed animals including a two-headed lamb and a butterfly and moth collection. I also never saw the collection of erotic pottery of the South American Moche and Chimu cultures.

Also, there were only a few minutes to see the galleries on the first floor filled with artifacts and displays relating to Rapa Nui. Unfortunately, all the labels were in Spanish, although I understand that tours are available in both Spanish and English.

I found the museum's most impressive display to stand outside the museum, a moai, one of the few original, ancestral figures created by the islanders not still remaining on the island. It is reputed to be only one of six moai removed from the island and now located elsewhere in the world.

Although it is reputed to be one of the smaller moai, seeing one of the original images from Rapa Nui was a highlight of the time spent on mainland Chile. Also, since very little material from Rapa Nui has been seen in any other museums visited around the world, it was very worthwhile to see a select few of the island's artifacts in the two museums visited in Santiago and its vicinity.

Adapted from:

http://www.vinadelmar.travel/tour/francisco-fonck-museum.html

https://www.lonelyplanet.com/chile/vina-del-mar/attractions/museo-de-arqueologia-e-historia-francisco-fonck/a/poi-sig/436008/363304

https://en.wikipedia.org/wiki/Viña_del_Mar

CHILE - RAPA NUI (EASTER ISLAND)

Country name: Republic of Chile (Spanish: República de Chile)

Site name: Rano Raraku

Location: Rapa Nui (also known as Easter Island; Spanish: Isla de Pascua)

UNESCO World Heritage Site: Rapa Nui National Park, no. 715, inscribed 1995

Tour Dates: 2-9 January 2009

Easter Island's Abandoned Moai: Rano Raraku

Hundreds of the ancient effigies sit like unseeing sentinels on its steep slopes on the remote island. Easter Island's Rano Rarako is the site of the largest number of the moai, the huge stone images carved by the islanders. It is regarded as the island's primary quarry and is where the tuff, a stone of compressed volcanic ash, was used for the creation of an estimated 95% of all the ancestral figures found on the island. It is thought that the quarry was used for some five hundred years and up until the early eighteenth century as the island's major source of stone for its famous images.

Rano Raraku's ancient name is said to have been *Maunga Eo,* meaning "fragrant hill." An aromatic plant is thought to have grown on the sides of the extinct volcano and to have permeated the air with its sweet fragrance.

It is one of seven main sites on the small, remote island known as Easter Island, also called Rapa Nui in the islanders' native language. Discovered by Dutch explorers on Easter Sunday in 1722, the island is reputed to be the world's most remote, inhabited island. Measuring only fourteen miles long and seven miles wide, the island sits out in the vast Pacific Ocean some 2,300 miles from mainland Chile and 2,500 miles from Tahiti.

Annexed by Chile in 1888, the island was given UNESCO World Heritage Site status as Rapa Nui National Park in 1995.

I had visited Rano Raraku with a local guide earlier, but the tour had been cut short by a rainstorm that had suddenly blown in from off the Pacific Ocean. With the assistance of helpful staff members at the small hotel in the village of Hanga Roa where I was staying, I managed to be able to hire a driver to take me out to the quarry site for another visit on my own. It was only on the second visit to Rano Raraku that I discovered many of the island's stone images, the moai, that I'm certain many visitors never are given a chance to see.

When I visited Easter Island in 2009, there was only an admission fee required at the site of Orongo, but I understand that now there is a ranger station at Rano Raraku where an entrance fee is collected.

On the earlier tour of the site, the guide had pointed to a stony path leading up a steep incline leading to the interior crater of Rano Raraku's ancient volcano. Coming over the rim of the volcano, I saw at least seventy more of the large statues sitting on the slopes of the caldera leading down to the fresh water lake inside the volcano.

Only when inside the crater could I appreciate its size, some 650m in diameter. In its center was a lake measuring from five to seven meters in depth and which was surrounded by totora reeds, called *nga'tu* by the islanders. The reeds, originally thought to evidence contact with South America, are now known to have been growing on the island for as least thirty millennia. It was also inside the crater that I discovered a herd of horses. Horses were also encountered elsewhere running free on the island. Many are rented to visitors to tour the island on horseback.

It was only later that I discovered that the crater of Rano Raraku is the site of an annual sporting event, Rapa Nui's *Tau'a*, an Easter Island triathlon. The event involves first crossing the lake in a canoe, then running halfway around it, and finally recrossing the lake by swimming on a board made of reeds.

Both inside and outside the extinct volcano the moai sit scattered about on its slopes, looking as though the ancient islanders had suddenly just walked away from the site. Carved face side up, many of the images look unfinished. Many are also half buried in the hillsides. Most of the figures follow a formula, with their large heads being about a third the height of the entire figure. Carved with prominent noses and recesses for eyes, the figures have spindly arms with long fingers clasp to their sides.

Since none of the moai at Rano Raraku ever reached the *ahu*, or platforms around the island for which they were intended, none have the eyes of coral and obsidian inserted into them. Only once on their *ahu* and with the eyes inserted were the images imbued with the spiritual power or *mana*, of the ancestors. Also most of the moai at the site have smooth backs and no special carvings on them except for one moai which has a ship with three square sails carved on its torso.

Rano Raraku is also the site of the so-called "El Gigante," meaning "the giant," a stone figure still lying unfinished in its site in the rock. If the image had been finished, it would have stood some 72 feet high and would have weighed over 160 metric tons.

By far, the most unusual figure at Rano Raraku is the so-called "Tukuturi" or "kneeling moai." Excavated by Thor

Heyerdahl in 1955, the figure is said to have astonished even the islanders since they had not known of its existence. The figure is tilted somewhat backwards and kneels with its hands on its knees in a posture called *tuku turi,* a pose used by singers in a ritual performed by the *Tangata manu* cult. Also, the figure has a raised head and is bearded. It is now thought possibly to have been one of the last moai ever to be carved.

Easter Island is, for me, one of the world's most important off-track sites to be visited. It is so remote. It is so enigmatic. It is a place so shrouded in mystery that I believe we will never know all of its secrets.

Adapted from:

https://en.wikipedia.org/wiki/Easter_Island

http://whc.unesco.org/en/list/715

https://en.wikipedia.org/wiki/Rano_Raraku

http://imaginaisladepascua.com/en/easter-island-sightseeing/easter-island-volcanoes/rano-raraku/

http://ourworld.compuserve.com/homepages/dp5/easter3.htm

CHINA

Country name: People's Republic of China
Site name: Great Wall, the western end
Location: Xinjiang Uyghur Autonomous Region
UNESCO World Heritage Site: no. 438, inscribed 1987
Dates of Visits: 19 September 2002; 25 April 2016

China's Great Wall: the West End

On my first trip to China in 2002, I found the Great Wall packed with many other tourists in spite of it being a chilly, overcast day. I could immediately see that it was one of China's most popular tourist attractions.

We had been taken to the Badaling section of the Wall, reconstructed in 1955 and located 70m (43 miles) northwest of Beijing. We were informed that the wall extending to our left was the easier climb; that to the right was the more difficult. Seeing that the wall to the right was almost devoid of other tourists, that was the section of the wall I chose to explore.

The climb was difficult but exhilarating. The views of the Wall as it twisted and turned over the mountainous terrain were awe inspiring. Almost before I realized it, the wall came to an end. As I peered over the rampart at the wall's end, I was amazed to see what were only ruins and often only the low outlines of the remains of the Wall. Only then did I realize that what I'd seen up to that point had been largely renovated or entirely rebuilt.

At the Wall's end was a lone merchant selling plaques with drawings of the Wall etched on them. I couldn't help but wonder if he would be selling anything that day due to the very few tourists I'd encountered on my trip on the Wall. I ultimately decided that I not only needed to give him at least one sale for the day, but one of his plaques of a shiny black material would make a fitting souvenir of my visit to the Wall. As a result, I still have the souvenir engraved with the date of my visit, 19-9-2002 (i.e., 19 September 2002), hanging on one of the walls of my apartment along with a display of other souvenirs from China that I call my own private "great wall of China."

Fourteen years later in 2016 while on the second trip to China, I had looked forward to seeing the other end of China's Great Wall, the western end. We were traveling in China's Xinjiang Uygur Autonomous Region when we were taken to the site of the Wall's western end marked with a boulder inscribed with UNESCO's logo and identifying the area as the location of sections of the Wall. It was initially disappointing that very little remained to be seen far out at the Wall's western end. Only very broken sections of the Wall remained, jutting up out above the shifting sands that continue to threaten to obliterate them. Not made of bricks or stone as found on the Wall's eastern end, out in the desert the Wall had been made of the local yellow, sandy soil sandwiched between layers of Jarrah branches. The overall effect of the Wall that remains is probably best described as being that of sections of a layer cake. It was only later that I learned that, unlike what I'd seen in 2002, much of the Wall had been built of a clay-rich soil call "loess" in a technique using rammed earth called *hangtu*.

Not being at all a single wall, but many different walls built centuries apart and sometimes parallel to each other, the Great Wall has traditionally been said to measure 21,196 km (13,171 miles) in length. Also, construction of the Wall is thought to have begun as early as the 7th century BCE. China's first emperor, Qin Shi Huang, is recorded as having added to the wall from 220-226 BCE, but little of his wall is thought to remain. Although repeatedly rebuilt and added to, most of what is seen today is dated as being from the Ming dynasty (1368-1644 CE).

Only later did I understand the true significance of the section of wall seen in 2016. It is now believed that the wall extends 500 km further to the west than originally thought. Rather than ending at Jiayu Pass in Gansu Province, it is believed that Emperor Wudi of the Han dynasty extended the Wall from Dunhuang to Yanze, present day Lop Nur. It must have been the Han dynasty extension of the Wall which we saw on our trip. Scenes of the Han dynasty construction project are said to be seen in frescoes in the Mogao Grottoes outside Dunhuang, a site we also visited on the trip.

Even with the newly discovered Han dynasty section of the Wall, it is now believed to have possibly extended even further to Kashi in the southeastern part of the Xinjiang territory.

Another site that was visited near that of the Wall was the so-called Small Fangpan Castle. This massive, rammed earth fortification sits forlornly on a flat, desolate plain, seemly out in the midst of nowhere. What was especially impressive was the massiveness of the earthen walls in sharp contrast to the small and cramped interior space. Looking like a huge cube, the massive ruin looks out over the desert landscape with a salt lake in the foreground and sand hills that look to stretch out into infinity in the distance. Described by the local guide as a "customs house," this huge fortification was also undoubtedly created for the protection of China's vast western frontier.

One myth about China's Great Wall that needs to be dismissed is that started as early as 1754 when it was claimed that the Wall could be seen from the Moon. The myth even appeared in 1932 in Ripley's "Believe It or Not." Actually the width of the wall even at a maximum of 9m would appear like a human hair seen from a distance of 3 km. Whether or not the Wall could be seen from a low Earth orbit is more controversial. NASA claims that it would be barely visible at an altitude of only 160 km (100 miles) and then only in the most ideal conditions. Others have said that it would be impossible to see the Wall with the naked eye unless the observer had a visual acuity seven times greater than normal.

Even in its most ruinous condition, China's Great Wall impresses when one realizes that it remains one of the largest constructions ever built by human beings.

Adapted from:

https://en.wikipedia.org/wiki/Great_Wall_of_China
http://whc.unesco.org/en/list/438
http://www.china.org.cn/english/2001/Feb/7996.htm
https://www.travelchinaguide.com/china_great_wall/
https://www.britannica.com/topic/Great-Wall-of-China

CUBA

Country: Republic of Cuba (Spanish: República de Cuba)

Site name: Fusterlandia

Location: Playa Jaimanitas, a suburb west of Havana (Spanish: La Habana), corner of Calle 226 & Ave. 3

Date of visit: 25 April 2017

A Cuban Fantasyland: Fusterlandia

Photographs and descriptions don't do him justice. The artistic genius of the Cuban artist, José Rodríguez Fuster, has to be experienced firsthand with a visit to Playa Jaimanitas, a small fishing village and suburb west of Havana.

Since 1975 José Fuster has covered nearly every available space of his property with mosaics made primarily from broken tiles in the brightest primary colors. Everywhere there are images of gauchos, amorous couples, boats, fish, various other sea creatures and abstracted female nudes. The prolific exuberance of the artist's creativity has also expanded outside the confines of his property into much of the small village of Playa Jaimanitas surrounding Fusterlandia.

Fuster has been characterized as the "Picasso of the Caribbean" and as a follower of the Catalan architect, Antonio Gaudí. Both designations are too limiting, I feel. While influences of Picasso and Gaudí are there, his work is highly unique in its own right.

If Fuster is to be categorized at all, he must be seen as a primitive, naïve, self-taught, and outsider artist. His work embodies a whimsy and childlike quality quite unlike the more sophisticated works of Picasso and Gaudí. His work also exhibits many of the characteristics of street and public art.

Unlike either Gaudí or Picasso, Fuster's works are primarily two-dimensional and limited to ceramics, tiles and mosaics. Some of his works, however, exhibit an excellence as pieces of sculpture in their own right.

Two of his large mosaic murals qualify, in my estimation as masterworks. One appears to be a representation of Noah's Ark and the other, a manifestation of the Virgin Mary, crowned as the Queen of Heaven and holding a small cross and the infant Jesus.

Although having exhibited primarily in Cuba, Fuster has also received international attention in exhibitions in Romania, India and England.

Admission to Fusterlandia is free, and it is still possible to see Fuster in person and to purchase original tiles created by him in his workshop.

Notable mosaics by other artists in Fuster's neighborhood include a large wall created as an homage to Antonio Gaudí, a large mural depicting Fidel Castro's arrival in Cuba from Mexico in this yacht, the "Granma," and another wall including a representation of the Mexican artist, Frida Kahlo.

Transportation to Fusterlandia is probably best arranged with one of the drivers of the classic car taxis in central Havana's Paseo del Prado. Taxi fares are cited as ranging from CUC$12 to CUC$15 with CUCs approximately equal to U.S.

dollars. Internet sites also state that transportation is available via public transport and by select hop-on/hop-off buses which are probably best used by more adventurous travelers and those conversant in Spanish.

The short visit to Fusterlandia was one of the highlights of the trip to Cuba and was definitely worth the special side trip outside central Havana.

Adapted from:

https://en.wikipedia.org/wiki/José_Rodríguez_Foster

http://www.huffingtonpost.com/regina-fraser-and-pat-johnson/havanas-fusterlandia-culturalart_b_1762925.html

https://www.lonelyplanet.com/cuba/havana/attractions/fusterlandia/a/poi-sig/1554872/358014

http://oncubamagazine.com/lights-shadows/jaimanitas-fusters-house-always-open/

http://www.atlasobscura.com/places/fusterlandia

EGYPT

Country name: Arab Republic of Egypt

Site name: Bibliotheca Alexandrina

Location: On the Mediterranean waterfront in Alexandria, Egypt

Tour Dates: 18 September - 1 October 2003

Egypt's Bibliotheca Alexandrina

The destruction of the ancient library is often cited as one of the greatest losses of knowledge in all of human history. Estimated to have contained anywhere from 40,000 to 400,000 papyrus scrolls, it is believed that not a single one has survived. It is seen as an irretrievable loss of ancient scholarship and learning.

Ancient Alexandria was not only the site of one of the largest and most important libraries of the ancient world, It was also a major, ancient cultural center. Alexandria is where Eratosthenes calculated the circumference of the world and where Aristarchus determined that Earth revolved around the Sun and not the opposite. It is where Herophilus determined that it was the brain that was the center of human thought and not the heart, and where Euclid devised his geometric formulas.

As usual, what I was erroneously led to believe as a student was that it was the Muslims that should be credited with the destruction of the great, ancient library. They're the bad boys of the Near East, so it's politically correct to blame such destruction on them. I imagined that the marauding Muslims stood at the railings of their ships anchored out in the Mediterranean and cheered as the great library went up in flames. I could imagine that they delighted in the great bonfire they had created as the flames reached skyward, hundreds of feet into the air and as the lurid flames grew into a great conflagration, destroying all the texts of the ancient infidels. If not in the Quran, of what use was any of the knowledge of the ancient Greeks and Romans, and especially that of any of the despised Christians?

So I was led to believe that the destruction of the library must have taken place in 642 CE when Amr ibn al-As and his Muslim army captured Alexandria. There also was the story that the library may have been destroyed much later in the 13th century by order of Caliph Omar Bar-Hebraeus.

It's best to fill young minds with oversimplifications and Western style propaganda. So I'd not known that when the library was actually destroyed and by whom remains highly controversial. There was no mention made of the siege of Alexandria by Julius Caesar in 48 BCE. or of the attack by Aurelian in the 270s CE. There was no mention of the Coptic Christian, Pope Theophilus, possibly destroying the Serapeum in 391 CE. It nevertheless appears to be agreed that at least by the time of Socrates of Constantinople, all the pagan temples as well as the smaller library at the Serapeum had been destroyed in ancient Alexandria.

I had just retired, and my first trip as a retiree was to Egypt. Also, I had treated myself to a new digital camera. I decided that I not only wanted to take the guided tour starting and ending in Cairo and that included a trip by riverboat up the Nile but that I wanted to take an extension of several days including a trip to Alexandria.

The young Muslim fellow that was our guide for the tour immediately said he would try setting up a tour of Alexandria for me. He said that he loved visiting Alexandria and that he'd welcome the chance to be my guide on the extension. Fortunately, the local tour company agreed to allow him to accompany me to Alexandria. They also set up an Egyptian driver, a large, burly fellow, that I discovered was a Coptic Christian and which I still believe must have been an off-duty Egyptian soldier or policeman. When I inquired why we took a trip to Alexandria through what I found to be a boring desert route, I was informed that a trip along the coast would have been too dangerous.

The local guide could not have been more accommodating. When I stated that I wanted at least a short stop at the new library of Alexandria, he immediately agreed. So I was permitted a photo stop at the new, ultra-modern library that today stands on the shores of the Mediterranean on what archaeologists believe is the site of the ancient library that no longer exists.

The idea of a new library commemorating the ancient one goes back to 1974. The site was selected that not only is where it is believed the ancient library stood but is between the campus of the University of Alexandria and the Mediterranean. Unfortunately, there is a very heavily trafficked street between the ultra-modern library as it sits glistening in the sun and the blue waters of the Sea.

Supported by President Hosni Mubarak as well as by UNESCO, a design competition generated over 1,400 entries. In 1988 the design of a Norwegian architectural firm, Snohetta, was selected. At a conference held in Aswan in 1990, USD $65 million was pledged, mostly from various Muslim countries. Ultimately costing an estimated USD $220 million, the new library was inaugurated in October of 2002.

The high cost of the vast architectural project has generated considerable criticism and charges that more was spent on the building than that set aside for the library's future contents. It has also been called a white elephant and a vanity project. Even so, the new library, a part of which appears to sit in a pool of water, is remarkable for its modernity. The slanted, circular, glass-paneled roof, much like an enormous sundial, is especially impressive.

One of the major features of the new library is its vast reading room measuring 20,000 square meters and is located on eleven, stepped levels. The circular reading room alone measures 160m in diameter and has a 32m high roof composed of glass panels. Its walls, composed of granite from Aswan, are engraved with inscriptions in 120 different languages.

The library complex also contains an archaeological museum, established in 2001 and which is the first of its kind in a major library. In addition, there is a conference center, four art galleries, a planetarium, a manuscript restoration laboratory and special collections of maps and multimedia. Making use of current technology, the manuscripts collection is reputed to have digital copies of over 6,000 rare books, maps, and other rare documents. The microfilm collection is said to contain copies of around 30,000 rare manuscripts and 50,000 other documents.

The library remains essentially trilingual with books mostly in English, French and Arabic. As of 2002, the library owned only 500.000 volumes. In 2010, the library was fortunate to receive another 500,000 books from the Bibliothèque nationale de France.

The British Library has contributed a microfilmed collection of about 14,000 manuscripts in Turkish, Arabic and Persian. There is also a large archive of Arabic and national newspapers.

Since the library relies very much on donations, it is estimated that it may very well take up to eighty years to fill its shelves. Not attempting to compete with other national libraries, the library is concentrating on materials relating to

Egypt, Islam, and the Near East. Even with space for five million books, the library remains relatively small, especially in comparison with the Library of Congress in Washington, DC, the world's largest, which is reputed to have well over 200 million volumes.

It may never reach the world-class status of other national libraries, but the new Bibliotheca Alexandrina remains a bold attempt to recapture the illustrious reputation of the ancient library founded by the Ptolemaic dynasty of ancient Egypt. Founded by Ptolemy I Soter, a Macedonian general and successor to Alexander the Great, I found it possible to imagine that the ancient library may have been visited by Cleopatra, and she may even have used the library to read some of its ancient papyri.

Adapted from:

https://en.wikipedia.org/wiki/Library_of_Alexandria
https://en.wikipedia.org/wiki/Bibliotheca_Alexandrina
https://www.bibalex.org/en/default
http://www.crystalinks.com/libraryofalexandria.html
http://news.nationalgeographic.com/news/2002/10/1016_021016_alexandria_2.html

ETHIOPIA

Country name: Federal Democratic Republic of Ethiopia
Site name: Tiya
Location: In the Soddo region, south of Addis Ababa
UNESCO World Heritage Site: no. 12, inscribed 1980
Date of Visit : 25 January 2011

Ethiopia's Mysterious Stelae at Tiya

Of all the awe-inspiring sites visited on the trip to Ethiopia, the field of stelae located outside the village of Tiya had to be among the most mysterious.

The thirty-six huge, ancient stone monoliths bearing strange carvings of swords and various other signs and symbols sit clustered in the tall grasses of a large field. Located less than 1 km. (.6 miles) outside the small town of Tiya to the south of Addis Ababa, the archaeological site was designated one of Ethiopia's nine UNESCO World Heritage Sites in 1980.

Tiya is regarded as the most important of the 160 archaeological sites in the Soddo region south of Addis Ababa.

The large stone stelae lie scattered about the site estimated at 200 square meters and enclosed in a barbed wire fence. The site can be entered through a large metal gateway. Thirty-two of the stone monuments are carved with images and symbols which have been almost totally undeciphered. The largest stela rises to an impressive height of 3.70m (over 12 ft.).

Joint venture excavations in the area by French and Ethiopian archaeologists have unearthed stone artifacts and skeletons of humans varying from 18 to 30 years in age. The stelae appear to mark mass graves and may be those of warriors. Carbon testing has dated the human remains to the 12th to 14th centuries CE. What ancient people created the stelae and what their purpose might have been, aside from the marking of graves, still appears uncertain.

The most common carvings on the stelae are the swords. It has been surmised that the number of swords carved on a stela may be indicative of the number of persons buried at the site. It has also been conjectured that the number of swords may symbolize the number of persons killed by a particular, buried warrior. Some of the swords on the stelae have been compared to the so-called "gallo" sword types of the Oromo, while other swords have been compared to traditional Somali daggers.

Some of the carvings appear to be representations of schematic humanoids. There are those who believe that the carved circles on some of the stelae may represent female breasts and may indicate that a nearby burial is that of a woman. Other carvings are thought to represent human body parts or tools.

Other carvings remain only as mysterious signs and symbols. A very common motif is the so-called "false banana tree" or "fountain-like" shape recalling to some extent the semi-circular forms found topping the stelae at Axum. Some stones also display a T-shaped symbol.

One stela fragment was seen the first full day of the trip, poorly displayed and dimly lighted in a dusty showcase inside the National Museum of Archaeology in Addis Ababa. What I believe to be the true masterpieces of the ancient Ethiopian stone carvers are the two stelae located outside on the museum grounds. Both are ornately carved with a plethora of swords and mysterious signs and symbols. The most remarkable of the two stelae is vaguely anthropomorphic in form. When visiting the museum, I strongly recommend that the two outdoor stelae are not to be missed.

Unfortunately, the studies of archaeological remains in Ethiopia have been few. Little research has actually been done at Tiya, and it has not been possible to identify the people responsible for the creation of the megaliths. There are some claims of finds of Middle Stone Age tools at Tiya and also evidence of tranchet blows on the stones that may date from the same time period. The most prevalent theory is that Tiya dates much later, from the 11th to 13th centuries CE.

The half-day trip from Addis Ababa to Tiya is best done with a local guide. The road to Tiya is one of Ethiopia's better black-top highways, and the entrance to the site, which is only approximately 400m from the main road, is easily identifiable by signs. An English-speaking, professional guide is usually at the site to admit visitors and to give tours during the day.

There appear to be some plans to upgrade the site and to make it a more developed, tourist-friendly site. There have also been plans to set up training for guides and instituting visits to other such sites in the area. At the time of our visit, it remained a very serene, undeveloped area.

A visit to the peaceful and bucolic site of Tiya with its enigmatic stelae was a most worthwhile excursion outside the often crowded and chaotic capital of Addis Ababa.

Adapted from:
https://en.wikipedia.org/wiki/Tiya_(archaeological_site)
http://whc.unesco.org/en/list/12
http://www.worldheritagesite.org/sites/tiya.html
http://www.bdnewsarchive.com/news/odetails.php?id=177538

GEORGIA

Country name: Georgia (Georgian: Sakartvelo)

Site name: Joseph Stalin Museum

Address: 32 Stalin Avenue 1400, Gori

Location: Gori, 86 km (53 miles) east of Georgia's capital, Tbilisi

Date of Visit: 21 September 2011

A Soviet Time Capsule: Georgia's Stalin Museum

According to sources consulted on the internet, little has changed since Soviet times in the city of Gori, Georgia. Also, little has changed in the city's star attraction, the Joseph Stalin Museum. Some say that, in Gori, it appears that the Cold War has never ended.

Joseph Vissarionovich Jughashvili, much better known as Stalin, was born in Gori on 21 December 1879. He spent his first four years in Gori until 1883 living in what has been described as a small wooden hut or hovel. Even then he lived in only the left half of the two room house. His father, a local shoemaker, rented half of the house while the owner lived in the other half. Stalin's father also used a basement room as his shoe shop. The house can still be seen in Gori today, enshrined under a pavilion with stately columns and located in front of Gori's museum dedicated to immortalize Stalin. Peering into one of the house's window, the one room in which the young Stalin lived looks very neat, prim and very much staged. A model of the house with the workshop in the basement is also on display inside the museum.

Also located in front of the museum is a statue of Stalin. It is not the one that has caused the most controversy in Gori, however. The larger statue still stands in front of the city hall in spite of having been removed clandestinely overnight in 2010. It was then reinstated on 20 December 2012 by Gori's municipal assembly which has many members that are still strong admirers of the man they view as being their illustrious native son. Plans were underway to move the large monument and its statue to the front of the museum as evidenced by the hole, complete with steel reinforcing, that had been dug, but it appears that move is still being delayed due to much controversy about the intended move.

Located in the city's central square, the Joseph Stalin Museum was officially dedicated in 1957. In 1989 it was closed, but then reopened. Today it remains Gori's primary tourist attraction and is even seen as a pilgrimage site by many who are still Stalin's admirers.

Nearly everything about the museum evidences its Soviet origins. Started in 1951, and before Stalin's death in 1953, it was ostensibly planned as a museum dedicated to the history of socialism. The reality is that it probably was always intended to immortalize Stalin. Designed as a monumental palazzo, the museum's façade possesses a long, arched colonnade. Inside, it is luxuriously furnished with marble floors, chandeliers and red carpeting. At the head of a marble stairway stands a statue of Stalin in front of a stained glass window.

Divided into six sections, the first room contains displays about Stalin's youth as a revolutionary as well as about his numerous imprisonments as a bank robber. The next room displays his rise to power and his becoming the Soviet Union's most powerful leader. Next, Stalin's role as commander of the Red Army during WWII is documented. In his victory over the Nazis, Stalin is portrayed as the godlike leader saving the Russian homeland from the diabolic Hitler. Subsequent galleries display gifts given to Stalin by various world dignitaries.

The most theatrically staged room is the one displaying Stalin's bronze death mask. In a darkened, columned rotunda painted black and with luxurious red carpeting, the death mask sits on a suitably highlighted pedestal. It has been said that the reverential staging is similar to that of Lenin's tomb in Moscow.

Plans were supposedly underway in 2008 to transform the museum into a "Museum of Russian Aggression," but maintaining the museum as is has been seen as essential to keeping its status as a tourist attraction and in bringing revenue into the city's coffers. As of December 2012, Gori's assembly voted to keep the museum as is.

So to this day, there are no mentions of the millions of people killed under Stalin's regime including thousands of the Georgian people. Nothing is said about the starvation of the Ukraine and the purges in the 1930s. Nothing is said about the 22,000 Georgians reputed to be KGB informers or that many of them were priests in Georgia's powerful Orthodox church.

Located outside and to one side of the museum stands Stalin's armored railroad train car. Weighing 83 tons, it was used by Stalin for traveling to the Yalta and Tehran conferences, since he reputedly had a fear of flying. The railroad car can be toured at an addition fee. The elegant interior contains bedrooms, a kitchen, bathroom with a shower and toilets, meetings rooms as well as a rudimentary air-conditioning system. In 1985 the railroad car was rescued from railroad yards at Rostov-on-Don and transferred to the museum.

Today, Stalin's reputation as a great statesman and world leader remains intact in Georgia's Gori. Still, there are those who have asked: What if Germany had such a museum dedicated to immortalize Hitler?

Adapted from:

https://en.wikipedia.org/wiki/
Joseph_Stalin_Museum,_Gori

https://www.theguardian.com/world/2015/aug/04/
georgia-stalin-museum-soviet-version-dictators-life-story

http://www.comtourist.com/history/stalin-museum/

https://en.wikipedia.org/wiki/Gori,_Georgia

http://wikitravel.org/en/Gori

GUATEMALA

Country name: Republic of Guatemala

Site name: La Democracia's "Fat Boys"

Location: La Democracia, Escuintla Department, Guatemala

Date of Visit : 15 November 2006

The Mysterious "Fat Boys" of La Democracia, Guatemala

Eleven of the strange, humanoid, monolithic figures called "Fat Boys" sit around two sides of the central plaza of the small town of La Democracia in the south of Guatemala. The twelfth figure sits at the entrance of the town's small archaeological museum, the Museo Regional de Arqueología de La Democracia.

Six of the sculptures depict human heads, while five represent humans with bodies. Also located at La Democracia is a sculpture in the form of a large receptacle or bowl.

Scholars have dated the sculptures as being 4,000 old. Two of the monoliths were originally located at the nearby site of Monte Alto, one a head and the other a human body. As a result,

La Democracia's figures have been classified as being pre-Olmec and to be from the so-called Monte Alto culture predating even the very early Olmec culture.

Carved from the local basaltic lava, the sculptures have received only a minimum of carving, accounting to some extent for their appearance of corpulence. Even the faces appear to be fat and bloated. Some say that the corpulence of the figures may have been considered a sign of affluence or beauty.

The figures also all appear quite generic and not representations of distinct individuals. Their spindly arms are tightly clasped around their large abdomens, and if they have feet, they are wrapped tightly around the bases of the figures. None of the figures bear any signs of gender. It has only been assumed that they are all male.

Discovery of the figures in 1976 is credited to a Dartmouth College geographer, Vincent H. Malmström. But one of the most astounding aspects of the figures was later discovered in 1979 by one of his field assistants, Paul Dunn.

It was Paul Dunn who discovered the magnetic qualities of the sculptures. As a result of his discovery, the figures at La Democracia are now regarded as being the world's oldest artifacts displaying magnetism.

What is even more astounding and perplexing is that the magnetism found in the figures appears to be localized. In the figures with human bodies, the magnetism has been found to begin to the left of the figure's navel and to exit to the right. In the heads, the magnetism begins at the right temple above the ear and exits below the ear. Such localized magnetism, it has been conjectured, may symbolize certain life forces. The magnetism at the navel may symbolize birth; that on the heads may symbolize cognition or knowledge.

Whether the magnetism of the figures was intentional or is merely circumstantial has been the subject of much debate. Regardless of whichever it might be, the magnetism of these strange figures appears to predate even the early Chinese experiments with magnetism by at least 2,000 years.

The figures at La Demeocracia only continue to mystify. What is their age? Who created them? What were they meant to signify? And most mysterious of all, what is the meaning and significance of their strange magnetic properties?

Sitting in the open air in the small town of La Democracia, the "Fat Boys" remain among the world's oldest and most mysterious artifacts created by prehistoric humans.

Adapted from:

https://en.wikipedia.org/wiki/La_Democracia,_Escuintla

http://www.messagetoeagle.com/enigma-of-the-ancient-magnetic-fat-boys-and-their-curious-magnetic-properties/

http://ancients-bg.com/the-magnetic-fat-boys-of-guatemala/

http://www.dartmouth.edu/~izapa/CS-MM-Chap.%203.htm

http://www.ancient-wisdom.com/guatemala.htm

INDIA

Country name: Republic of India

Site name: Mausoleum of Itimad ud-Daula

Location: Agra, Uttar Pradesh; located on the east bank of the Yamuna River, approximately 4 km from the Taj Mahal

Protected by the **Archaeological Survey of India**

Date of Visit: 4 April 2013

Mausoleum of Itimad ud-Daula:
A Mughal Architectural Jewel Box

Many visitors to India are probably driven right past it in their rush to see the Taj Mahal in Agra. Others, such as myself who was at the time a first-time visitor to India back in 2004, hadn't even heard of it. When I inquired about it after seeing a roadside sign with its name, I was told by a local guide that it was only a "copy" of the Taj Mahal.

Later, after learning more about it from guidebooks, I was gratified to see it listed on the itinerary of a subsequent trip to

India in 2013. Our trip itinerary said it might be included on our visit to Agra "if there was time."

Not wanting to miss seeing it the second time, I pleaded with our guide to be able to see it if at all possible. In her perfect Queen's English, she quickly assured me that we definitely would visit it. She even added that it was one of her all-time favorite examples of India's Mughal architecture. Finally being able to see the Mausoleum of Itimad ud-Daula, I found it even to exceed my already high expectations.

The Mausoleum of Itimad ud-Daula is often called a "jewel box" of Mughal architecture as well as a "draft of the Taj Mahal." It is also often called the "baby Taj," a term I object to since I feel it diminishes its importance as one of Mughal India's most magnificent monuments. While I admit that it does not have the grandeur and the magnificent scale and proportions of the Taj, in many respects I feel it surpasses the Taj Mahal in its attention to the most minute and exquisitely detailed decoration.

The mausoleum's strange name, Itimad ud-Daula, means "pillar of the state." It was an honorific title given to Mirza Ghiya Beg, an Iranian emir in exile. In addition to having served the emperor Akbar, he was made vizier or prime minister after the marriage of his daughter, Nur Jahan, to the emperor Jahangir in 1611. He held the title of Lord Treasurer until his death in 1628 in Agra. It was his daughter, Nur Jahan, who built the mausoleum for her father as well as for her other relatives from 1622 to 1628. Although her father's mausoleum was built in Agra, her tomb and Jahangir's were built in Lahore.

It is obvious that there is much about the mausoleum that serves as a prototype for what is today regarded as one of the world's greatest architectural masterpieces, the Taj Mahal. Like the Taj Mahal, it sits on the eastern bank of the Yamuna River in Agra. Its overall ground plan is, like the Taj Mahal, that of a garden tomb. It possesses a surrounding wall inside of which is a garden separated into four quadrants marked by water channels and walkways. It possesses a monumental entry gate of red sandstone with decorative details in white marble. It also possesses subsidiary buildings at its sides as well as the one behind it sitting on the river's edge.

In comparison with the Taj Mahal, it is much more modest in size, with a square ground plan measuring twenty-three meters on each side. Sitting on a platform some fifty meters in size and about one meter high, the mausoleum possesses hexagonal towers measuring thirteen meters high at each of its corners. Unlike many other Mughal monuments, the mausoleum has no dome. Instead, it is topped by a square structure with a pyramidal roof crowned with lotus pedals and finials.

Inside the mausoleum are interconnecting passageways surrounding the central chamber. In its exact center sits the cenotaph of Asmat Begam, while in the corner rooms are the cenotaphs of Nur Jahan's daughter, Ladli Begum, and those of other relatives.

The mausoleum's "jewel box" reputation is confirmed by its being called the "most gorgeously ornamented Mughal building." Its exterior decoration is a prime example of *horror vacui*. Almost every available surface is filled with the most exquisite decoration. In addition to geometrical patterns there are stylized floral motifs, arabesques, and representations of such objects as cypress trees, wine bottles, vases containing bouquets, cups, dishes and various flowering plants. There are also inscriptions from the Quran on the sixty-four exterior panels on the mausoleum's ground floor and twelve interior panels on the pavilion above.

Its reputation is even further enhanced as being the first Mughal building covered completely by white marble quarried in Rajasthan. Its *pieta dura* decoration uses inlays in its white marble background of such semi-precious stones as topaz, lapis lazuli, onyx, jasper and cornelian. Totally lacking is any glazed tile work, with all the mausoleum's decoration in either inlay as on the exterior or painted as in the building's interior.

Adding to the intricate detail of the mausoleum are the delicately carved, pierced marble, *jali* window screens that admit light into the mausoleum's dim interior.

Many scholars have compared Itimad ud-Daula's decoration to that of contemporary ivory carving and to the intricate designs of Mughal manuscript illumination. They have also compared its decoration to that of adjacent, ancient Iran and have theorized that the mausoleum reflects the sophisticated artistic taste of the Iranian emir for which the mausoleum was built.

Unlike the Taj Mahal, the Mausoleum of Itimad ud-Daula has yet to receive an inscription as a UNESCO World Heritage Site, but at least it has received protection from the Archaeological Survey of India.

My very strong recommendation is that, when visiting Agra, you should not fail to visit this masterwork of Mughal architecture.

Adapted from:

http://en.wikipedia.org/wiki/Tomb_of_I'timād-ud-Daulah

gra.nic.in/historyof_ITMAD-UD-DAULA.html

http://www.remotetraveler.com/tomb-of-itmad-ud-daulah-agra/

http://asi.nic.in/asi_monu_tktd_up_itimaduddaula.asp

INDIA

Country name: Republic of India

Site name: Masrur

Location: 32 km from Kangra, 60 km from Dharmsala, Himachal Pradesh, India

Citations: Declared a national monument in 1914

Date of Visit: 27 March 2013

India's Mysterious Masrur

Little is known about the ruined temple site of Masrur. There are very few known facts about its date and about who may have constructed the magnificent temple site.

Masrur is reputedly locally known as Himalayan Pyramid and Thakuwada, meaning "Vaishnavite temples." It is located near Kangra and Dharmsala in the Himachal Pradesh of northern India. The temple complex can be quite easily reached by car. It is still quite remote and is seldom visited by foreign tourists but is visited with some frequency by the local people. When the site was visited in 2013, there were no visitor amenities and no signage giving information about the site. That may have changed due to plans to promote the site as a tourist destination and to make it more visitor friendly.

Masrur was discovered by Europeans in 1875 and written about first in 1913 and again in 1915. It has since been declared a national monument in 1914 and tentatively listed for designation as a UNESCO World Heritage Site. Currently it is cared for under the auspices of the Archaeological Survey of India.

Only conjecture and legends surround Masrur. While it has been compared to such well-known rock-cut temple sites as those at Ellora and Mamallapurum, it remains a very rare rock-cut site for northern India. Rock-cut sites are more rare than sites built of individual, quarried pieces of stone. There are many difficulties in carving monolithic, natural rock outcroppings. Rock-cut sites of sandstone such as that of Masrur entail coping with fault lines and variations in the hardness of various rock strata.

Unfortunately much of Masrur's sculptural decoration has been obscured by weathering, defacing and earthquake damage. making it difficult to identify the deities to which the temples were originally dedicated. Some historians believe Masrur was originally Shaivite. Images of Rama, Lakshman, Sita, and the image of Shiva in the center of the lintel of the main temple have so far been located.

Also questionable are the number of temples originally carved at Masrur. Some authorities say there were nineteen. Today only fifteen remain at the site covering a rocky ridge measuring 48m long by 105m wide (159 by 105 feet). The temples are said to be in the *nagara* style and are of the northern *shikara* or temple tower type. The highest temple tower has been measured as rising 24m (80 feet) above the temple floors. There are rock-cut stairways on either sides of the main temple that adventurous visitors can climb to the tops of the temples.

The magnificent temple complex has suffered much from defacement, weathering and the earthquake of 1905. Also, some of the finest, surviving sculptural panels have been removed from the site and are now preserved in the state museum in Shimla. Erotic sculptures are said to have been found at Masrur, but if such is true, I did not see them.

Dates for the temples have been suggested, but only on a stylistic basis. Although some have dated Masrur to the 7th century, most authorities date it to the 8th to 9th centuries and primarily to the late 8th century, based on its affinities to India's classic Gupta style. Also due to the lack of any inscriptions, there are even fewer suggestions as to what wealthy patron must have been responsible for commissioning such a sophisticated, rock-cut temple complex. One conjecture is that Masrur was commissioned by a ruler of the ancient Jalandhara kingdom of the Punjab plains. There is also the legend that the Pandavas of the *Mahabharata* built the temples.

In spite of its ruinous state, Masrur remains very impressive as it stands on the high point of a rocky ridge overlooking the surrounding landscape. Its location provides superb vistas of the Dhauladhar Mountain Range and the Beas River valley.

Making the site even more impressive is the rock-cut reservoir, measuring 25 by 50 meters, carved from the local sandstone and standing in front of the temples. For this visitor, the reflections of the monumental, ruined temples in the placid waters of the artificial lake made Masrur appear even more mysterious and magical

Until more research reveals much more about Masrur, it remains one of India's most enigmatic, ancient temple sites.

Adapted from:

https://en.wikipedia.org/wiki/Masroor_Rock_Cut_Temple
http://www.atlasobscura.com/places/masrur-temple
https://www.intltravelnews.com/2016/01/indias-masrur-rock-cut-temples
http://www.atlasobscura.com/places/masrur-temple
http://123himachal.com/temple/masroor.htm

INDONESIA

Country name: Republic of Indonesia
Site name: Candi Sewu
Location: Central Java, 800 meters north of Prambanan
Tour Dates: 3-15 April 2005

Candi Sewu: Indonesia's Second Largest Buddhist Temple

Candi Sewu, meaning "a thousand temples," is Indonesia's second largest Buddhist temple. It is little known and seldom visited. Tourists flock to see central Java's magnificent Buddhist temple of Borobudur and the monumental Hindu temple of Prambanan. But few visitors to Indonesia even know about the Buddhist temple located nearby that predates them both.

Dated by inscriptions, Candi Sewu predates Prambanan by over seventy years and Borobudur by about 37 years. Discovered in 1960, one inscription dates Candi Sewu to 782 CE while the so-called Manjusrigha inscription dates it to 792 CE.

While on the trip to Indonesia, I had already visited both Borobudur and Prambanan, each on two separate occasions and

51

with different local guides. As a result, I asked one of the local guides if she would take me to visit the group of ruined temples that stood near Prambanan. She expressed surprise at my request, saying that she had never had another foreign visitor express any interest in visiting the other temples. She agreed to be my guide in visiting them but said she would have to consult her notes to be able to tell me much about them.

Candi Sewu was the first of the temples we visited on our half-day tour. I remember very well that she had to contact a caretaker to open a locked gate to allow us to enter the fenced-off temple complex. Once inside, we had the vast, very ruinous temple area all to ourselves.

Other smaller temples in the area that we visited later were Candi Bubrah and Candi Gana, both thought to have been guardian temples for Candi Sewu. Other temples in the area such as Candi Lor and Candi Kulon have only a few stones remaining. Before the construction of either Borobudur or Prambanan, Candi Sewu is thought to have been the area's major temple with the smaller temples in the area arranged around it in the form of a *mandala* symbolizing the Buddhist universe.

While the present temple complex's name is Candi Sewu, meaning "thousand temples," its original name is thought to have been "Manjusri grha," meaning house of Manjusri. In Mahayana Buddhism, Manjusri is a bodhisattva symbolizing "transcendental wisdom" or "gentle glory." Resembling the layout of Prambanan in some respects, the temple complex is composed of only 279 structures rather than the thousand suggested by the temple complex's present name, with 240 of the smaller structures being guardian or *perwara* temples arranged as a *mandala* around the other major temples.

Candi Sewu's rectangular temple grounds measure an impressive 185m from north to south and and 165m from east to west. The temple complex has four entrances at the cardinal points that were once guarded by twin *Dvarapala* statues. The main temple measures 29m in diameter and 30m in height.

Made of andesite stone, the main temple forms a 20-sided cross-shaped polygon. The temple has a taller central chamber with four lower chambers forming a cross. It is thought that the large lotus pedestal in the central chamber may have once held a bronze image of the bodhisattva, Manjusri.

Hundreds of ruins continue to lie around the site, and even then, many of the original stones are missing. During the Java war, many stones were carried away and used for fortifications. Many of the Buddhist images have been decapitated and the heads stolen. Dutch colonists took images away to be used as garden ornaments; villagers used stones as construction material, and many sculptures and reliefs were taken away and are now in foreign public and private collections.

Restoration work has been ongoing at Candi Sewu since the early 20th century, but much still needs to be done. The reconstructions of the main temple and two side temples were completed in 1993 and inaugurated by President Soeharto the same year. But in the Yogyakarta earthquake of 2006, the temple complex was severely damaged with the central temple suffering the most. Metal supports had to be used to prevent the temple's collapse. It has been reported that the main temple, initially closed, has since been repaired and reopened to visitors.

It is hoped that restoration and reconstruction will continue at Candi Sewu and that this magnificent example of Javanese Buddhist architecture will become much better known and appreciated by more visitors to Indonesia's central Java.

Adapted from:

https://en.wikipedia.org/wiki/Sewu

http://www.revelations-of-the-ancient-world.com/candi-sewu-prambanan-java-indonesia/#

http://asiaforvisitors.com/indonesia/java/central/yogya/candi-sewu/index.php

http://www.photodharma.net/Indonesia/24-Candi-Sewu/24-Candi-Sewu.htm

IRAN

Country name: Islamic Republic of Iran (formerly Persia)
Site name: Gonbad-e Qabus
Location: City of Gonbad-e Kāvus, province of Golestān
UNESCO World Heritage Site: no. 1398, inscribed 2012
Date of Visit: 16 May 2014

Iran's Enigmatic Tower: the Gonbad-e Qabus

Iran's Gonbad-e Qabus had been on my wish list of destinations for nearly four decades. It had been back in 1966, while an art history graduate student at the State University of Iowa, Iowa City, that I had selected the Iranian tower as the subject of my master's degree thesis. As a naïve, young student, little did I realize what a formidable task I had taken on in attempting an analysis of the tower and in evaluating all the legends and myths that had grown up around it since its construction in the early 11th century CE.

As a result, I was elated to discover that it would be possible to extend my tour to Iran in 2014 to visit the tower located in the northeastern section of Iran and close to the border with Turkmenistan.

Starting from Tehran, it had taken nine hours to reach the modern city of Gonbad-e Kavus, located in Golestan Province in northern Iran and east of the Caspian Sea. While riding through a typical Iranian city, we suddenly stopped. Only then, looking high up out of the window, did I realize we had arrived at our destination.

Standing tall and alone on a low artificial hill in a park, the Gonbad-e Qabus is a huge tower, reputed as being the world's tallest structure built exclusively of unglazed, fired brick. Rising 236 feet, including its platform, the so-called "Dome of Qabus" is a tapering cylinder with ten-foot-thick walls and ten equally spaced right-angled flanges that form a decagon. At the base on the tower's eastern side, is an entrance topped by a window grill. In the conical roof there is a small window also facing east. Otherwise, the tower is a solid mass of unglazed brick. Its only decorations are the two bands of inscriptions, located between the flanges at two separate levels.

The Arabic inscriptions in the Kufic style are made of fired brick and are part of the fabric of the tower. Those making the bricks obviously had difficulty forming the Kufic text in that it does not match the sophisticated brickwork of the rest of the structure. The inscriptions state that the tower was commissioned by the Ziyarid Amir, Shams al-Ma'ali Qabus ibn Wushmgir. They also give the dates of 397 of the lunar Hegira and the year 375 of the solar Hegira, corresponding to 1006-1007 CE. It is therefore Iran's earliest building bearing its own date of construction.

The inscription duplicated at two levels on the tower's exterior mentions the tower as being a "kasr," also often transliterated as "qasr." The term is usually translated as meaning "castle." The term has, as a result, been used to identify the tower as being the final resting place or "castle" of Qabus.

There has been no evidence, however, of any burial having been found during any of the investigations undertaken within or outside of the tower. Russian excavations in 1899 revealed that the tower's walls extend thirty-five feet below the interior's ground level, and they uncovered no burial site. An elderly man at the site stated that he remembered that there had been a deep pit in the center of the floor inside the tower which has since been covered over with cobblestones.

Even with the halogen lights installed inside the tower, it remains a very dark and inhospitable space if it had ever been intended to be lived in. The interior has been built with solid brickwork and with no stairway or with form of access to its top. No significant amount of light enters the tower through the roof's very small window. One can see only a dark void when looking up inside the tower. The only openings to the tower's interior are the small grill over its doorway and the small roof window. Rather than having symbolic significance, it is thought that the roof window may have been created merely for the ventilation of the tower's interior.

The primary legend associated with the tower is ascribed to what appears to be an elusive, Iranian historian named al-Jannabi. Eventually a reference to him was found as having visited both Mecca and Medina in 1556 CE. It was also discovered that his full name is Abu Mahammed Mustapha Ebnol Saiyed Hasan al Jannabi and that he had been born at Jannaba, a city in ancient Persia not far from Shiraz. He is credited over and over again in the literature and in descriptions of the Gonbad-e Qabus with initiating the legend that Qabus was encased inside a glass coffin and hung by chains from the top of the tower's interior. Similar descriptions of such burials have been associated with both Alexander the Great and the Biblical prophet, Daniel. It seems especially noteworthy that his legend about the burial of Qabus materializes some five and a half centuries after the construction of the tower.

Unfortunately, no concrete evidence has been found to substantiate any such legend for Qabus or for either Alexander the Great or the prophet Daniel. No evidence appears to have been found that anything remains at the top of the Gonbad-e Qabus's interior except for solid brickwork. It has also been impossible to determine if the tower has any form of double dome or possibly that there is only an empty space between its inner ceiling and outer conical roof.

Without any evidence at all of the tower having been used as a place to commemorate a burial, the best explanation for the construction of the tower is that suggested by the authorities at the Gonbad-e Qabus World Heritage Base in Gorgan, Golestan Province. They believe that Qabus built the tower primarily to glorify and immortalize himself. If so, it has been over a millennium that the tower has been a prominent landmark on a major overland trade route. It is largely because of the tower that one ever hears of the Zayarid Dynasty and its amir living in the early 11th century.

It therefore appears that Qabus built for himself a highly original architectural masterwork that had no historic precedent at the time. If he built it as part of his legacy and to survive the vicissitudes of time, he did very well.

The Gonbad-e Qabus became a protected site back in 1930 with the enactment of Iran's National Heritage Protection Act. In 1975 it was cited by the Iran Cultural Heritage, Handcrafts & Tourism Organization. In 2012, it was designated a UNESCO World Cultural Heritage Site.

After standing on its hill for over 1,000 years, the tower has finally been recognized as a major example of world architecture. The influence of the Gonbad-e Qabus has also extended into the 20th century as seen in the open-work tower built in 1954 atop the mausoleum of the famous Persian philosopher, Avicenna, located in Hamadan, Iran.

Adapted from:

https://en.wikipedia.org/wiki/Gonbad-e_Qabus_(tower)
http://whc.unesco.org/en/list/1398
https://www.tripadvisor.com/ShowUserReviews-g672704-d6993882-r360758093-Gonbad_e_Qabus_Tower-Gonbad_e_Kavus_Golestan_Province.html#

ISRAEL

Country name: State of Israel

Site name: Second Temple Model

Location: Israel Museum, located in the Givat Ram neighborhood of Jerusalem

Date of Visit: November 2008

Jerusalem As Jesus Saw It

I had seen all the usual sites of Jerusalem such as the Church of the Holy Sepulchre, the Garden of Gethsemane, the Garden Tomb and the Via Dolorosa. Still I had no concept of what Jerusalem may have looked like during the time of Jesus until I visited the Israel Museum, located on Ruppin Road, not far from the Knesset.

Most visitors to the Israel Museum concentrate their attention on the Shrine of the Book where the Dead Sea Scrolls are exhibited without realizing that nearby is a scale model of the city of Jerusalem. It represents Jerusalem as it would have appeared in the 1st century CE during the Late Second Temple

Period. At that time, it is estimated that the city would have covered over 450 acres.

Only by chance did I discovered the large scale model of the magnificent Second Temple as expanded by King Herod the Great and built on the site of Solomon's temple that was destroyed by the Babylonians in 587 BCE. The model shows the city in the year 66 C.E. and before it would be sacked and the temple destroyed after a nine month siege by the Romans on 29 August 70 CE.

The city of Jerusalem in miniature has been scaled at 1:50 and covers 2,000 sq. meters (21,520 sq. ft.). The model was built by Michael Avi-Yona, an archaeologist and a leading scholar on the history of Jerusalem between 1962 and 1966,. He based the model on such Jewish sources as the Mishnah and on the writings of the first century CE Jewish historian, Flavius Josephus. He also used finds from excavations in Jerusalem and other contemporaneous Roman cities.

Dedicated in 1966, the model was first located at the Holy Land Hotel in the Bayit Vegan section of Jerusalem. It had been commissioned by the hotel's owner, Hans Kroch, as a memorial to his son, Jacob, who had died in the battle over Kibbutz Nitsanim during the War of Independence.

When it was realized that the model had become such a tourist attraction and important cultural object, in 2006 the model was separated into over one-hundred parts and transported to the Israel Museum where it was reassembled. It is now a permanent part of the Museum's 20 acre grounds where it is continually updated based on new archaeological findings.

Today the model remains the best place to see Jerusalem as Jesus may have seen it in the first century CE.

Adapted from:

http://www.imj.org.il/en/wings/shrine-book/model-jerusalem-second-temple-period

https://en.wikipedia.org/wiki/Israel_Museum

ISRAEL

Country name: State of Israel
Site name: Tel Aviv's White City
Date of Visit: November 2008
UNESCO World Heritage Site: no. 1096, inscribed 2003

Tel Aviv's White City

If you think Israel is important primarily for its ancient sites, think again. The architecture of one of Israel's nine UNESCO World Heritage Sites dates from the early 20th century.

Having just arrived at the Ben Gurion airport outside Tel Aviv, I found that I had an afternoon at leisure before rushing off to see such ancient sites as Capernum, Qumran and Masada. Fortunately, I had an Eyewitness Travel guide to *Jerusalem and the Holy Land* that mentioned Tel Aviv's so-called White City, designated a UNESCO World Heritage Site in 2003.

Founded in 1909, Tel Aviv was built north of the walled port city of Jaffa under the British Mandate of Palestine from 1917 to 1948. Since then it has become a vibrant urban metropolis and the major economic center of Israel. Commissioned by Tel

Aviv's first mayor, Meir Dizengoff, the architect and city planner, Sir Patrick Geddes, was given the job of laying out the new city which essentially provided him with a blank slate for trying out new ideas in architecture and urban design.

Designed and built by immigrant architects from Europe from the early 1930s until the 1950s, Tel Aviv is reputed to have over 4,000 buildings in the new Bauhaus or International Style. The Bauhaus, for which the style was initially named, was an architecture, art and design school in Germany from 1919 to 1933 led by such notable founders of the modernist movement as the architect, Walter Gropius.

The architectural style's emphasis on simplicity and functionality was considered appropriate for the socialist ideals of the Zionist movement giving rise to the founding of the new city of Tel Aviv. Simple, functional design was seen as allowing quick, and inexpensive construction. Much of the new architecture was built with reinforced concrete, and characteristics of the new style included plain, unadorned, and asymmetrical façades of white stucco with ribbons of horizontal strip windows. Vertical stacks of windows. often called "thermometer" windows lighted the stairwells.

Transferring an architectural style from Europe to the desert and Mediterranean climate required a number of adaptations. White was found to reflect light and heat; large glass areas were replaced by smaller, recessed windows and were shaded by overhangs; pitched roofs were replaced with flat ones, and narrow balconies allowed residents to sit outside and catch breezes from the Mediterranean. Buildings raised on pillars or *pilotis* allowed winds to blow under buildings and created ground-level play areas for children.

The three major zones of Bauhaus style buildings are the central White City area, the Lev Hair and Rothschild Avenue area and the Bialik area. The area also is defined by Allenby Street to the south, Begin Road and Ibn Gvirol Street to the east, the Yarkon River to the north, and the Mediterranean to the west.

Wandering from my high-rise hotel located on the waterfront of the Mediterranean, I found the largest concentration of Bauhaus buildings on Tel Aviv's Rothschild Boulevard and the neighboring Ha'am Street. Rothschild Street was found to have central garden areas, kiosks, and benches, while Sheinkin Street was more commercial with boutiques and cafés.

I never did find the Bauhaus Center located at 99 Dizengoff Street where I would have found books, souvenirs and information relating to Bauhaus architecture. I learned later that the center runs weekly guided tours. Plans are also underway for a White City Heritage Center for promoting architectural preservation to open in the Max-Leibling House on Idelson Street in 2018.

Fortunately, I found a book in the bookstore of the Yad Vashem **Museum** while in Jerusalem: *Bauhaus Tel Aviv; an architectural guide*, by Nahoum Cohen with photographs by Jachin Hirsch (London: Batsford, 2003. 276p).

It's recommended that you wear comfortable shoes for a lot of walking, and be prepared to see many buildings in a sad state of repair, although there are efforts currently underway to renovate many of the deteriorating buildings. You'll not see such a large concentration of Bauhaus/International Style architecture anywhere else in the world.

Adapted from:

https://en.wikipedia.org/wiki/White_City_(Tel_Aviv)
http://whc.unesco.org/en/list/1096
www.bauhaus-center.com/
https://www.touristisrael.com/the-white-city-tel-aviv/344/
http://www.visit-tel-aviv.com/white-city-tel-avivyafo#.WW54FkvpUnE
https://www.amazon.com/s/ref=nb_sb_noss?url=search-alias%3Dstripbooks&field-keywords=Cohen%2C+Nahoum.+Bauhaus+Tel+Aviv

JAPAN

Country name: State of Japan (Japanese: Nippon or Nihon)

Site name: Horyuji

Location: 7.5 miles outside of Nara

UNESCO World Heritage Site: no. 660, inscribed 1993

Date of Visit: 21 July 2005

World's Oldest Wooden Structures: Horyuji, Japan

There were three sites in Japan that were not on the itinerary of my tour in 2005 that I wanted very much to visit. One was the monumental, bronze image of the seated Buddha at Kamakura. Since then I was privileged to see the image of the Unification Buddha in South Korea in 2015 which is the larger of the two. I had also wanted to see one of Japan's holiest Shinto shrines, the Ise Grand Shrine. But access to it is strictly limited, and it is largely obscured by the four-foot wall that surrounds it.

The third site I wanted to see was the Buddhist temple complex of Horyuji, located 12 km outside of central Nara. Since I had an extra day at leisure in Japan, I decided to attempt to see

Horyuji on my own. Little did I realize what an adventure it would become.

Earlier I had managed to find my way to the National Museum in Tokyo. but although what I saw there was most worthwhile, I totally missed seeing the 300 objects donated to the imperial household by Horyuji in 1878 that are displayed in a separate building at the museum.

Since I was staying in a hotel in Kyoto, I found that I first had to take a train to Nara. Then I had to change to another train on the *Yamatoji* Line to the railway station at Horyuji. Getting off at the station, I found that there was no Buddhist temple in sight. Fortunately, a helpful Japanese fellow who understood my confusion motioned me to follow him. Pointing me in the right direction past a group on small shops, I ultimately came upon a long, broad, tree-lined sidewalk. In the distance I saw the Great South Gate, rebuilt in 1438, of the western section of Horyuji, the *Sai-in*. I had finally arrived at the site of the world's oldest wooden buildings and the area containing Japan's earliest Buddhist monuments. I had arrived at Japan's first, inscribed UNESCO World Heritage Site. As early as 1993, Horyuji, along with Hokki-ji had been declared a UNESCO site.

Founded by Crown Prince Shotoku in the 7th century CE, the temple was built in honor of the prince's father and dedicated to Yakushi Nyorai, the Buddha of healing. The name, Horyuji, is said to mean "Temple of the Flourishing Law" while another name, Horyu Gakumonji means "Learning Temple of the Flourishing Law." At the time of the temple's construction in 607 CE, the temple complex was called by yet another name, Ikaruga-dera.

Only later did I find that Horyuji had two main areas and that I'd only found it possible to visit one of them. Just as I was ready to leave the site, I happened to notice a building I'd not visited. It was the Gallery of Temple Treasures built in 1998 to display part of the ancient temple's vast collection of works of art. Fortunately, I finally found the large building's entrance facing the back of the building near the eastern section of the temple complex. Needless to say, I was in awe of the excellence of the art on exhibit in the building's galleries.

Most of my time spent at Horyuji was devoted to the western or *Sai-in* area. The eastern section, the *To-in*, with its octagonal Hall of Dreams or *Yumedono* Hall, located 122m to the east was the area I totally missed. I also failed to realize the full extent of the site that also contains quarters for monks, libraries, as well as lecture and dining halls. I later discovered that the entire area designated a UNESCO site located in the Nara prefecture covers forty-eight ancient wooden buildings located at the two sites of the Horyuji and Hokki-ji temples. The temple of Horyuji covers 14.6 hectares while the smaller temple of Hokki-ji covers .7 hectares.

Not only are many of the structures at Horyuji the world's oldest wooden buildings, they are considered masterpieces of wood construction. Using a post-and-lintel system, intricate series of brackets transfer the weight of the heavy, tiled roofs to the huge supporting columns. The buildings at Horyuji are also notable for the entasis of their columns and for the cloud-like forms of the brackets supporting the roofs.

The western section of Horyuji contains the central gate or *Chumon*, the main hall or *Kondo*, and the pagoda of five stories. All have been dated to the Asuka period (538-710 CE). Although there is controversy over what exactly was destroyed in a fire of 670 CE, most of the buildings have survived basically intact. They have undergone numerous renovations over the many centuries, however, with repairs being made in the 12th century CE and then again in 1374 and 1603 CE.

Entering the western area's main gate, I first encountered two of Japan's oldest *Kongo Rikishi*, a pair of huge, fearsome figures guarding the gate. The most prominent structure once inside the western precinct is the five-story pagoda, standing at 32.45m (122 feet) in height and measuring 20 by 20m in width. It is the pagoda that has been dated as one of the world's oldest wooden buildings. Dendrochronological research on its central pillar points to a date of 594 CE. At the base of the pillar extending three meters below ground level, a fragment of a bone of the Buddha is reputed to be enshrined. Not intended to be climbed, the pagoda contains four scenes depicting the life of the Buddha pointing out in the four cardinal directions.

Next to the pagoda stands the *Kondo*, also regarded as one of the world's oldest wooden buildings. The great hall measures 18.5m by 15.2m and has been built in two stories. The first story was provided with a double roof supported by added columns in the later Nara Period. Although damaged in a fire of 1949, it is believed that fifteen to twenty percent of the original building survives.

Among the very important, early Buddhist images at Horyuji is the so-called Shaka Triad, dated to 623 CE in which Sakyamuni is flanked by images of Bhaisajyaguru and Amitabha. There is also the Yakushi Nyorai, dated from before the fire of 670 CE. Then there is the notable Yumedono Kannon measuring over six feet in height and made of gilded wood, thought to have been intended as a representation of Prince Shotoku, the temple's founder.

After visiting Horyuji, I could see that only a half day visit was inadequate. Planning on spending a full day at the site would have allowed much more time to appreciate its many ancient buildings and hundreds of temple treasures.

I was surprised that I was the only Westerner at the site on the day of my visit and that there was only one bus in the temple's parking area. Such a great national treasure as Horyuji seemed so sadly neglected by so many foreign travelers.

Adapted from:

https://en.wikipedia.org/wiki/Hōryū-ji

http://whc.unesco.org/en/list/660

http://www.horyuji.or.jp/horyuji_e.htm

http://www.japanvisitor.com/japan-temples-shrines/horyuji-temple

http://www.ancient.eu/Horyuji/

JORDAN

Country name: Hashemite Kingdom of Jordan

Site name: Petra Church

Location: On the ridge northeast of Petra's colonnaded street

UNESCO World Heritage Site: Petra was designated a
UNESCO site in 1985, no. 326

Date of Visit : 22 April 2006

The Byzantine Mosaics of the Petra Church

I had wanted to take the local guide up on his offer of an optional tour to the so-called "Little Petra" on our extra half day spent at Petra, but no other tour members were interested. So I decided to return to Petra's main site on my own.

The day before, at the location of an ancient tree, the guide had pointed to a path leading up a rocky ridge and has stated that several early Christian churches had been excavated in the area north of Petra's central city area.

Trudging up the narrow path, I encountered a very modern space frame structure. Inside were the excavated remains of one of Petra's Christian churches, the so-called Petra Church. Time was limited, so I never did find the other two churches further up the path, the Blue Chapel and the Ridge Church.

I learned later that, to protect the excavated church area from the sun, wind, and water, the innovative space frame structure designed by Shutler Architects of Arlington, VA, had been installed over the site by Starnet International Corporation of Longwood, Florida. I also learned that the excavations had begun in 1996 under the aegis of the American Center of Oriental Research in Amman.

The Petra Church has been dated to Petra's Byzantine period and to around 450 CE. Discovered in 1990 by Kenneth W. Russell, the triple aisled church was found to have been dedicated to the Virgin Mary and probably served as the city's cathedral. Built over what were earlier Nabatean remains, the church has an atrium paved in stone with a central cistern for storing water which can still be seen today. To the west, there is a baptistry with a cross-shaped font, another structure in the area that I failed to see.

The Petra Church suffered a fire in the 7th century CE, but it did not totally destroy the remarkable cache of historic, ancient papyrus scrolls found in a cabinet in the church's storeroom. Discovered in 1993 were 152 scrolls written primarily in a cursive Greek. The historic find is now regarded as the largest collection of written, ancient documents ever found in Jordan. Discovered in the many documents were records of marriages, births, business transactions, wills, and tax records.

It was the basilica of the church that drew most of my attention. Although it is only the lower level of the church that has remained, it could be seen that the church's main building had a wide nave paved in marble as well as narrower side aisles. At the eastern end was a broad central apse bordered by smaller side apses.

What was most remarkable of all were the beautifully preserved and expertly detailed floor mosaics of the side aisles. Secular in their subject matter, it has been conjectured that sacred images had not been used so they would not be walked upon by the church's congregation. The subjects of the mosaics included mythological subjects, various forms of plant and animal life, objects such as baskets and vases, decorative medallions, and shell-like, semicircular forms, most of which had been enclosed in decorative borders.

Having always regarded Petra as being a Nabatean site later absorbed by the Roman Empire, I was surprised to learn that it also had an important and illustrious history as the site of a thriving early Christian community. I was especially gratified to be able to see such a remarkable collection of Byzantine style mosaics in such an unexpected place.

Adapted from:

http://www.seetheholyland.net/tag/ridge-church/

http://www.art-and-archaeology.com/jordan/petra/pchurch/pc05.html

http://eilat-petra.com/the-church/

KAZAKHSTAN

Country name: Republic of Kazakhstan

Site name: Tamgaly Archaeological Park

Location: In the Chu-Ili mountains, Almaty Oblast, ca. 170 km northwest of Almaty

UNESCO World Heritage Site: no. 145, inscribed 2004

Date Visited: 7 October 2005

The Petroglyphs of Kazakhstan's Tamgaly Gorge

There are estimated to be not just hundreds of petroglyphs at the Tamgaly Gorge but thousands -- some 5,000 in fact. It is said that it is "the most striking site of rock arts in Central Asia." and that its "unique images and the quality of their iconography sets them apart from the wealth of rock art in Central Asia."

Tamgaly is said to mean "painted or marked place" in Kazakh and other Turkic languages. Located in the arid Chu-Ili mountains, the petroglyphs are clustered primarily in forty-eight areas and are thought to date from the second millennium BCE to the early 20th century. The Chu Ili mountain spur at the western end of the Tienshan Mountains is the location of the gorge created by the Tamgaly River. It is an area with springs and vegetation unlike the mountains on the border of Kazakhstan with Kyrgyzstan and the arid central Kazakhstan plains in the north.

The site includes Mount Tamgaly, 982m in height. Running through the center of the area is the Tamgaly River flowing to the plains to the north. Located in the gorge are black rock faces that rise in stages. It appears to have been an area that attracted pastoral communities since the Bronze Age.

Five sites contain the largest concentrations of petroglyphs, estimated at some 3,000. Located on the surfaces of the local rock, the most impressive and best preserved petroglyphs have been created by a technique of incising the images on the rock with stone or metal implements. Most prevalent are the wide variety of animals. Also of much interest to archaeologists are the images of zoomorphic creatures, abstracted forms of people and what appear to be solar deities. It is thought that some of the petroglyphs may represent a pantheon of gods with representations of dancers, women giving birth, and groups of worshippers. Especially controversial are the so-called "sun-head deities."

The largest number of petroglyphs are thought to date from the Bronze Age with a smaller group dating from the Iron Age. There are also glyphs dating from the Middle Ages as well as from more modern times. That the area was a place of burials is evidenced by the area's many box-like enclosures or cists and the mounds of earth or kurgans dating primarily from the Middle to Late Bronze Age.

Unfortunately, little protection is being given to the petroglyphs. The site is accessible only by private transportation, and there is no entrance fee. A lone soldier may be found at the entrance, and the old signs in Russian give little information about the site. It is therefore very difficult to understand much about the site without a knowledgeable guide or a guidebook.

In 2001 Tamgaly was inscribed as a Property of National Significance on the List of Monuments of History and Culture. In 2003, it was designated as the State Archaeological Reserve of Tamgaly under the auspices of the Ministry of Culture of the Republic of Kazakhstan. In 2004 it received UNESCO World Heritage status.

I had seen many ancient petroglyphs elsewhere when traveling, but I'd never seen such a profusion of petroglyphs nor such a variety of different types of images. In spite of the expert explanations of our local guide, I could still only wonder what symbolism many of the images must have held for the ancient people who created them.

Adapted from:

http://en.wikipedia.org/wiki/Tamgaly
http://whc.unesco.org/en/list/1145
http://www.worldheritagesite.org/list/Tamgaly
http://culture360.asef.org/organisation/state-archaeological-reserve-museum-tamgaly/

KOREA (South Korea)

Country name: Republic of Korea (South Korea)

Site name: Unification Buddha, also known as the *Tongil Daebul*

UNESCO Designation: Seoraksan National Park designated a biosphere reserve in 1982.

Location: On Mount Seoraksan in Sokchu, Gangwan Province

Date of Visit : 17 October 2015

World's Largest Seated Buddha Image: South Korea's Unification Buddha

If it were size alone, the image of the Buddha located in South Korea's Seoraksan National Park would be impressive. The image itself measures 14.6m (48 ft.) in height and sits atop a pedestal 4.3m (15 ft.) high. The overall height of the image is 18.9m (62 ft.) excluding the separate nimbus or halo attached behind the Buddha's head. The immense figure is estimated as weighing 108 tons.

South Korea's Unification Buddha is said to be the world's largest bronze image of the seated Buddha, surpassing the large Buddha image located in Kamakura, Japan. The image depicting Amida Buddha in Japan dating from 1252, but later rebuilt, measures 13.35m (43.8 ft) in height.

The Unification Buddha sits in a beautiful, bucolic setting of one of South Korea's national parks. The large number of Koreans in upscale hiking gear encountered on the day the park was visited attested to the fact that it is one of the country's most popular sites for hikers. The very long, difficult climb along a paved walkway just to the site of the image was in itself very taxing to say nothing about the climb further up the mountain to the temple beyond, the Sinheungsa (also spelled Shinheungsa). Itself a very important site to visit, the Sinheungsa is the head temple of Korean Buddhism's Jogye Order.

The Seoraksan National Park was listed as a nature preserve in 1965 and cited as a biosphere reserve by UNESCO in 1982. Designated a national park in 1970, the reserve measuring 163.6 square kilometers contains many of South Korea's mountain peaks as well and many rare plant and animal species.

Completed in 1997, the Unification Buddha was financed by over 300,000 donations from worshippers visiting the temple for over a decade. It is estimated that the cost of the image was 3.8 billion won or approximately 4.1 million USD. The hollow bronze image is reputed to contain the original Buddhist scriptures, the *Tripitaka*, as well as three fragments of the Buddha's robe, the latter donated by the Myanmar government. In addition to containing the relics of the Buddha, the image was created to express the yearning of the Korean people for the unification of their country.

Seated in the lotus position of meditation with crossed legs, the figure's face possesses partially closed eyes and a somewhat enigmatic smile. In the image's forehead is a third eye of amber inset with a center of jade. Clad with a robe covering only his left shoulder, the figure's hands are depicted in a *mudra* symbolizing the Buddha's enlightenment.

The giant figure is seated on a lotus flanked by sixteen panels recounting the path of the Buddha toward enlightenment through the help of various Bodhisattvas. Altars in front of the image hold lighted candles purchased by worshippers from nearby shops.

It was only later that I discovered an underground temple located at the back of the giant image. A series of steps led down to a temple dedicated to the thousand-armed Avalokitesvara, the Bodhisattva of compassion also known as Guanyin in China and Kannon in Japan.

I had always regretted not finding it possible to visit the giant Buddha image in Japan on my trip in 2005, so I especially appreciated seeing the large image in South Korea.

Although much later in date and different in style, it mirrors in many respects all the essential and traditional elements of the much earlier but somewhat smaller image in Japan.

Adapted from:

https://en.wikipedia.org/wiki/Sinheungsa

https://www.360cities.net/image/unification-buddha-sinheungsa-temple-seoraksan-national-park

LAOS

Country name: Lao People's Democratic Republic

Site name: Plain of Jars

Location: Central plain of the Xiangkhoang Plateau, Laos

UNESCO designation under consideration

Date of Visit : 16 January 2007

Laos's Mysterious Plain of Jars

Thousands of the large, enigmatic, stone jars lie scattered across the central plain of Laos's Xiang Khoang Plateau. The huge jars lie in groups of one to around four hundred on the plateau located at the end of Southeast Asia's principle range of mountains, the Annamese Cordillera. On my first trip to Laos, I found it possible to visit two of the major sites where groups of the jars are located. Located not far from the Laotian village of Phonsavan, the first area was the more easily accessible. Since my visit, a visitors center has been opened in August of 2013 giving information about the prehistoric site in English as well as about the history of the area during the war of 1964-1975.

The second site was reached only after following a narrow footpath, crossing a bamboo bridge, passing through several rice paddies, and climbing over a stile built over the fence around the site. It was the more picturesque of the two sites, being located on a low hill covered by shade trees.

Varying in size from one meter to three meters in diameter, the stone jars have been made primarily of sandstone, while others have been identified as having been hewn from limestone, granite and a stone conglomerate. Although there are regional differences in the forms of the jars, most are larger at the bottom than at the top. Most possess lips at their tops which are thought to indicate that the jars were designed to have lids. Few stone lids have been found, however, and none have been discovered left covering the jars. It is thought that, if the jars had lids, they may have been made of perishable materials or carried off and reused elsewhere.

Some stone discs have been found, usually having one flat side. Rather than functioning as lids for the jars, they are though to be grave markers and as coverings of burial pits. Few such discs have been found, especially in comparison to the number of jars.

Several quarries, usually not far from the clusters of jars, have been identified. It is conjectured that iron chisels were used for carving the huge jars. All the jars found are undecorated with the exception of one jar located at Site 1, where a vaguely anthropomorphic, so-called "frog man" has been carved on the jar's side.

Some remains of bones and teeth displaying signs of cremation have been found inside the jars. Otherwise the jars are totally empty or filled only with remains of rainwater and debris.

Most archeologists have dated the jars to the Iron Age and to 500 BCE to 500 CE. The French archaeologist, Madeleine Colani, working in the 1930s, theorized that the jars were part of prehistoric burial practices. Findings of remains of humans, fragments of pottery, stone and glass beads, iron and bronze objects, pieces of charcoal, and various other burial materials supported her theories. Unfortunately, little further archaeological research was done at any of the sites until 1974 when Site 1 was finally mapped. Again, discoveries lead to the belief that the burials at the site were contemporaneous with the date of the jars.

Research also led to the conjecture that the jars might have functioned as primary or secondary burials and as the burials of important individuals. Other human remains found at the sites may have been those of persons of lesser importance. It has also been thought that the jars may have been used for a form of ritual decomposition before the bodies were cremated and a secondary burial was performed. The jars may have been used as funerary urns where the deceased would have been first buried in a fetal position along with personal ornaments and other goods. Regarding the age of those whose remains have been found, many have proved to be adolescents.

A natural limestone cave found at Site 1 with manmade holes in its roof have led some researchers to believe that it had been used as a crematorium, with excavations done by Madeleine Colani supporting the theory. Our local guide stated that the cave had also been well known as a hideout of the Vietcong and the Khmer Rouge, accounting for the many bomb craters in the area.

Studies of the locations of the groups of jars has led researchers to believe that many were located on low rises in the plains, providing views over the surrounding countryside. It has also been thought that the groups of jars may have been formed in conjunction with ancient trade routes, and especially in relation to the salt trade.

Among the various legends that have grown up about the use of the ancient jars is one that maintains they were used for the collection of rain water. The most common legend involves a legend about a warrior king named Khun Cheung. He is believed to have created the jars for the making of a rice beer or rice wine in order to celebrate his victories over enemies. Other legends have maintained that the jars were not of stone but from materials made into a stone-like mix that was then fired in a kiln such as might have been located inside the cave at Site 1.

When visiting the two sites, we were warned by our local guide to remain only on marked paths. We were informed that the U.S. Air Force had dropped more bombs on the area in Laos than during the whole of WWII. Included in the many bombings were 262 million anti-personnel cluster bombs, 80 million of which have never exploded. As a result, many areas are still off limits and are still filled with bomb craters and unexploded bombs. Many of the jars were either destroyed or displaced. At one point while visiting the second site, I became uneasy when I found there were no more marker stones in the area in which I found myself. Later, after visiting the sites of the jars, we were taken to a location in the nearby village of Phonsavan where there were displays of remains of land mines and photos of those who had been maimed by unexploded ordnance (UXO).

On a subsequent visit to Laos, I was very surprised to discover, in the capital city of Vientiane, one of the jars sitting to one side of the temple of Haw Pha Kaew. A local guide said that it had been brought to the temple grounds by helicopter. In spite of appearing to have been pieced together from stone fragments, the lone jar still gave those on the guided tour some idea of the immense size of the jars.

Much is still unknown about the enigmatic stone jars that are scattered over the plains of Laos. Perhaps UNESCO World Heritage status for the plains area would allow more archaeological research on the mysterious, prehistoric jars.

Adapted from:
https://en.wikipedia.org/wiki/Plain_of_Jars
http://www.lonelyplanet.com/laos/northern-laos/plain-of-jars/introduction
Thepsimuong, Bounmy. The Plain of Jars; a guide book. Vientiane, 2004.

MEXICO

Country name: United Mexican States (Spanish: Estados Unidos Mexicanos)

Site name: Parque - Museo de La Venta

Location: Near Villahermosa, Tabasco, Mexico

Tour Dates: 29 November - 11 December 2004

Mesoamerica's Oldest Culture: the Olmecs

The Olmecs are considered to have been the oldest, major, pre-Columbian culture of Mesoamerica. Their civilization is often referred to as the "cultura madre" or "mother culture" of Central America. Their culture has been thought to have provided the basis for such other pre-Columbian cultures as those of Teotihuacán, the Mayans, and the Aztecs.

It is therefore most unfortunate that one of the primary sites of the Olmecs, that at La Venta, has been in large part destroyed by the building of an oil refinery at the site's southern end and making additional archaeological excavations unlikely.

On the other hand, it is fortuitous that many of the artifacts found at La Venta have been transferred to an archaeological park near Villahermosa, the capital of the Mexican state of Tabasco. Set along pathways cut through a jungle-like environment are four of the colossal heads for which the Olmecs are so justifiably famous. Located within the park are also numerous other Olmec figures as well as several of the so-called altars or thrones upon which are seated what are thought to be rulers observing sacred rituals or ceremonies.

The Olmec culture has been divided into three phases: Early Formative (1300 to 900 BCE), Middle Formative (900-400 BCE), and Late Formative (400 to 200 BCE). In addition to La Venta, other sites identified as being Olmec have been located at San Lorenzo, Tres Zapotes and El Manatí. San Lorenzo is regarded as being the earliest and is thought to have declined at about 900 BCE, with La Venta then becoming the center of Olmec civilization. With outlying areas at such a location as San Andrés, La Venta was probably primarily a civic and religious center with large plazas, pyramids and sacred areas for rituals and ceremonies.

Although one of the large Olmec heads had already been seen in the large archaeological museum in Mexico City, the Museo Nacional de Antropología, it was a pleasure to see four other such monumental heads at the park of La Venta. Thought to represent Olmec rulers, the colossal heads with their strangely upturned lips wear what almost appear to be football helmets. Weighing many tons and sometimes measuring up to 2.84m (9 ft, four inches) in height, the gigantic, monolithic heads have been identified as having been quarried over 80 km away from the basalt of Cerro Cintepec in the Tuxtla Mountains.

The Olmecs remain very much a mystery, having disappeared over 2,000 years ago, and much about their culture has been irrevocably lost. On the other hand, it is believed that much of the mysterious Olmec culture remains in its profound influence on other, later, Central American, pre-Columbian civilizations.

Walking along the shaded pathways cut through the jungle of the park and encountering the strange Olmec sculptures was not the only reason for the ominous feeling I received white visiting the La Venta archaeological park. At the end of the tour, a large, black jaguar was to be seen pacing back and forth in its cage in a small zoo. As the huge, muscular beast eyed me, I couldn't help but think I must be seen as a likely prospect for lunch. That it is was a melanistic example of the jaguar species, appearing almost totally black, made it all the more an awesome sight.

Adapted from:

https://en.wikipedia.org/wiki/La_Venta

https://www.tripadvisor.com/Attraction_Review-g249850-d538149-Reviews-Parque_Museo_La_Venta-Villahermosa_Central_Mexico_and_Gulf_Coast.html

https://www.thoughtco.com/the-olmec-city-of-la-venta-2136301

MOROCCO

Country name: Kingdom of Morocco

Site name: Majorelle Garden

Address: Avenue Yacoub el Mansour, Marrakesh, Morocco

Date of Visit: 10 June 2010

A Garden Oasis: Majorelle Garden, Marrakech

This beautiful garden may not be all that far off the tourist track, but I found it to be a most welcome respite from the chaos of Morocco's Marrakech. The garden seemed so peaceful and serene, especially after having been hassled and harassed by Marrakech's hawkers, vendors, performers, and especially by the very persistent street urchins. I had just come from the Jemaa el-Fnaa, the city's huge public plaza that has become overly crowded with entertainers, sellers of touristy trinkets, and other tourists. Although quite well known as a popular, local attraction, I hadn't found it possible to visit the garden while on an earlier trip to Morocco back in the 1980s.

Covering almost two and a half acres, the Majorelle Garden is reputed to contain approximately three hundred different species of plants from five of Earth's continents. I found its collection of exotic cacti to be especially impressive. Raised pathways cut through plantings of banana trees, coconut palms, stands of bamboo and plots of bougainvillea. Also, there are fountains, ponds and water channels filled with lilies and lotus blossoms.

The feast for the senses continues with the sweet aromas of many flowering plants and sounds of resident birds. Flying about the garden are such species as robins, sparrows, blackbirds, warblers, great tits, bulbuls, and turtledoves. In addition to the calls of the birds, there are also the calming sounds of splashing fountains and of water flowing down the channels running through the plantings.

The creation of the garden was started in 1924 by Jacques Majorelle (1886-1962), the son of an Art Nouveau cabinet-maker from Nancy, France. Majorelle was a watercolor painter, and although his paintings are on display in the museum inside the garden, he is known primarily for the magnificent garden he created in Marrakech. He is also known for the intense, deep, cobalt blue he used so often in painting various features of the garden as well as its buildings. The special shade of blue has become so famous as to become known as "bleu Majorelle" or Majorelle blue. For forty years Majorelle worked on creating his garden masterpiece.

In 1964, the property was purchased by the fashion designer, Yves St. Laurent and his partner, Pierre Bergé. Together they worked to restore and preserve the garden and its buildings. When Saint Laurent died in 2008, his ashes were scattered in the garden. A monument in the form of a broken columns sits in a secluded and sheltered section of the garden in silent memory of the renowned designer.

Today, the original art studio of Majorelle houses the Berber Art Museum, a collection of approximately 600 artifacts created by Morocco's indigenous people. Included are carpets, textiles, musical instruments, examples of traditional dress as well as items crafted of wood, metal and leather. Unfortunately, the museum was closed at the time of my visit.

On the other hand, a small shop was open selling coffee-table style books and souvenirs. Also open was a small café selling drinks. In addition, a small galley was open displaying greeting cards and letters that Saint Laurent had created to send to friends as well as other small works of art.

The garden has been open to the public since 1947, and today it is maintained by a local ethnobotanist, Abderrazak Benchaâbane.

Set off from the rest of the so-called "Ochre City" of Marrakech by a high garden wall, a walk down the garden paths bordered by the brightly painted pots filled with plants or a rest stop on one of its benches are certain to provide a calming retreat from the chaotic city within which the Jardin Majorelle is located.

Adapted from:

https://en.wikipedia.org/wiki/Majorelle_Garden
http://jardinmajorelle.com/ang/
http://www.lonelyplanet.com/morocco/marrakesh/sights/parks-gardens/jardin-majorelle
http://jardinmajorelle.com/ang/visiting-the-garden/
http://www.gardenvisit.com/gardens/majorelle_garden

MYANMAR

Country name: Republic of the Union of Myanmar (formerly Burma)

Site name: Yangon's Indian Town Mosques

Location: Central Yangon

Tour Dates: 12-27 December 2005

Yangon's Indian Town Mosques

For a country so predominantly Buddhist, I found Myanmar's major city, Yangon, remarkably cosmo--politan. While sightseeing in the city on my own, I was surprised to find a group of mosques concentrated in a section of the city often referred to as "Indian Town" or "Little India."

Yangon, formerly known as Rangoon, was the country's capital up until November of 2005 when a new capital was built far to the north at Naypyidaw. Yangon, with its population of over 5 million, still remains the country's largest city and its economic and cultural center.

Ever since the 1600s, the city has had an influx of foreigners including the Portuguese, Dutch, Chinese, Indians, and above all, the British. Today, almost none of the British remain in Myanmar, but there are many that remain that are of mixed ancestry and that often regard themselves superior to the other Burmese people because of their English ancestry.

It was primarily during colonial times and under British rule, when the country was called Burma, that several waves of immigrants came from India to Yangon. Today the area around Anawratha Street is usually regarded as the center of city's the Indian population.

The Buddhist temple, the Sule Pagoda, located in the center of a roundabout in the city's center, stands in the midst of what is often called "India Town" by Yangon's residents. Down one street off the roundabout, I encountered the Shree Shree Krishna Shiva Temple, located on Maha Bandoola Street. Finding it open to the public. I discovered that it had an impressive array of Hindu images along with a few that were Buddhist.

It was in the opposite direction from the Sule Pagoda that I discovered the largest collection of the city's mosques. In and around Yangon it has been estimated that there are about ninety mosques. Government surveys have claimed that Myanmar's population is only about four percent Muslim. Muslim leaders say that the figure is far too low, and they estimate the country's Muslim population as high as twenty percent. It is also said that almost any sizable town in Myanmar has at least one mosque.

In such a country as Myanmar, Buddhism takes precedence, so support of the mosques comes mostly from wealthy Muslim businessman and from private donations.

Yangon's best known and most popular mosque is the Masjid Sunni Bengali, located in the very heart of Yangon along Sule Pagoda Road. I found it very near the famous Traders Hotel and not far from the Scott Market (aka the Bogyoke Market).

Among other mosques that I found it possible to photograph was the Cholia Jame Masjid, built by Muslims from Madras in 1869. I was also elated to meet an elderly gentleman at another mosque who graciously invited me into the building so I could photograph the magnificent dome on the interior, decorated with painted arabesques.

Aside from the mosques' minarets, pointed arches, and many copulas and turrets, I usually found little that would qualify as being distinctly Indian in style. Most of the mosques were in a style that seemed unique to Myanmar. Only the so-called Surti Masjid seemed somewhat more Indian in style.

Most tourists will only be guided to the Buddhist monuments in and around Yangon. So my chance discovery of the mosques of Yangon was very much one of my most worthwhile off-the-tourist-track adventures during my second trip to Myanmar in 2005.

Adapted from:

https://en.wikipedia.org/wiki/Islam_in_Myanmar

http://myanmarmuslimtour.blogspot.com/p/mosque-in-myanmar.html

http://thecinnamonjourney.blogspot.com/2012/05/little-india-at-yangon.html

http://wikitravel.org/en/Yangon

Country name: Republic of Peru

Site name: Islas Palomino

Location: Six miles from the port of Callao and west of the island of San Lorenzo

Date of Visit: 10 September 2007

Island Wildlife Sanctuaries: Peru's Islas Palomino

I am usually not very enthusiastic about excursions during which the major attraction is wildlife. But the half-day trip out into the Pacific Ocean to the small rocky islands of Islas Palomino was an awesome experience and a highlight of the trip to Peru.

Departing from the historic port of Callao to the south of Lima, the trip out to the islands took only about one hour. Sometimes called "Lima's little Galapagos," the small islands are less well known than the Islas Ballestras located near Pisco further to the south. The Islas Palomino are far less touristy as a result, and on the day of our trip out to the islands, we appeared to be the islands' only visitors.

The two major islands in the group are San Lorenzo and El Frontón. San Lorenzo is Peru's largest Pacific island, while El Frontón was once the site of a notorious prison. It was out to the west of San Lorenzo that we began to see the wildlife for which the small islands are so well known.

It was first on San Lorenzo that we began to see large colonies of migratory birds. The wide variety of bird species that can be seen on the island include cormorants. gulls, guanaves, boobies, pelicans, and Inca terns. It was also on San Lorenzo that we saw colonies of Humboldt penguins. The Humboldt current, rising from the Antarctic, cools the waters running along the western coast of South American and makes it possible for the Humboldt penguins to live in what is otherwise a tropical region.

Further out in the Pacific we soon heard the barking and smelled the stench of the sea lion colonies. On many of the jagged outcroppings of rocks were hundreds, if not thousands, of sea lions. It often appeared that every possible square inch of the rocky islands was occupied by a sea lion. The islands even appeared to be a living, moving mass of sea lion bodies. Not only were the islands alive with the sea lions, but the ocean surrounding the islands were alive with hundreds of them.

Why the islands have no predators is not totally understood. But it is obviously the lack of predators that is the primary reason the small rocky islets have attracted so many of bird species and the enormous sea lion colonies.

It was especially the sheer size of the sea lion colonies that boggled the mind of this traveler on his trip to Peru.

Adapted from:

https://en.wikipedia.org/wiki/Palomino_Islands_(Peru)

http://enperublog.com/2009/06/02/islas-palomino-boat-trip-in-callao/

SRI LANKA

Country Name: Democratic Socialist Republic of Sri Lanka (formerly Ceylon)

Site: Gal Vihara

Location: Polonnaruwa, Nissankamallapura, Sri Lanka

UNESCO World Heritage Site: no. 201, inscribed 1982

Date of Visit: 19 October 2010

Masterworks of Buddhist Art:
Sri Lanka's Gal Vihara

Even the impressive full-color photographs in the travel literature and guidebooks didn't prepare me for my visit to the site of the Gal Vihara in Sri Lanka.

It was my fifth day visiting Sri Lanka. We were visiting the country's second most ancient city, Polonnaruwa, located in the Cultural Triangle in north central Sri Lanka and one of the island nation's seven UNESCO World Heritage Sites.

Located in the northern section of the vast archaeological site of ancient Polonnaruwa, the Gal Vihara, meaning "stone shrine"

is also referred to as the "Kalugal Vihara" or the "Black Stone Shrine." At the site are four colossal, rock-cut Buddhist images. Reputed to be constructed in the 12th century by King Parakramabahi I, the four images originally had their own enclosures and had been carved out of the face of a large outcropping of granite.

The images are said to be part of Parakramabahi I's northern monastery. On the rock face between the rock-cut cave and the image of the standing Buddha is one of ancient Sri Lanka's longest inscriptions. In it, Parakramabahi describes his reforming of the Buddhist religion and outlines a new ethical code for monks.

Two of the colossal figures carved out of the cliff face are seated images of the Buddha in the lotus or meditative pose of *dhyani mudra*. The larger image, measuring 4.6m (15 feet) in height, sits under an arch with smaller images of the Buddha looking down from celestial temples and possibly evidences Mahayana Buddhist influence. The niches containing lions and the crossed symbols of the *vajra* may also evidence Tantric symbolism.

The smaller, seated image of the Buddha, also in *dhyani mudra*, measuring 1.2 m. in height (4 feet), now sits in a carved recess closed off by a metal grille.

The most famous image at the Gal Vihara is the reclining Buddha, measuring 14 m. in length (46 feet). depicting the *parinirvana* of the Buddha. It is one of Sri Lanka's most iconic images and is also among the largest images in all of Southeast Asia. Especially notable is how the Buddha's head makes a subtle depression on the pillow that has been placed under his head. Both the end of the pillow and the soles of the feet of the image are decorated with lotus blossoms.

The standing image measuring nearly 7 m. in height (23 feet) is the most enigmatic. Many scholars maintain that it is not an image of the Buddha at all. With arms crossed across his chest, a highly unusual gesture for an image of the Buddha, it may be an image of Ananda, a disciple of the Buddha, whose sad expression depicts grief at the *parinirvana* or death of the Buddha. Other scholars have discredited the theory and maintain that it is an image of the Buddha, since other Buddha images have been found in a similar pose.

All four images of the Buddha have been admired for the artful way in which the natural strata of the rock has been used to such a great advantage in the carving of the images.

Today the magnificent images at the Gal Vihara are among those most often visited Buddhist images in Sri Lanka. They are considered among the supreme masterworks of the ancient Sinhalese stone carvers.

The visit to the Gal Vihara was a major highlight of the trip to Sri Lanka and contributed much to making my tour of the fascinating island country one of my best trips ever.

Adapted from:

https://en.wikipedia.org/wiki/Gal_Vihara

http://whc.unesco.org/en/list/201

http://www.buddhanet.net/sacred-island/gal-vihara.html

https://lanka.com/about/attractions/gal-vihara-polonnaruwa/

TAIWAN

Country name: Republic of China (Taiwan)

Site name: Shung Ye Museum of Formosan Aborigines

Location: Taipei, Shinlin District; located 200m diagonally across from the National Palace Museum

Date of Visit : 8 October 2015

Taipei's Museum of Indigenous Culture

Visiting this small, ethnographic museum was such an unexpected pleasure after having had one of the worst guided museum tours ever at the nearby National Palace Museum in Taipei, Taiwan.

The National Palace Museum, renowned as one of the world's foremost collections of Chinese art, was chaotic and thronged with local Chinese visitors. I was also dismayed to see how poorly the museum's priceless treasures were displayed. The primary reason I had added Taiwan to my trip to South Korea was to see the Palace Museum's collection, and the museum tour we were given proved to be only one of the worst fiascos of the trip.

I was also very disappointed to find that photography inside the museum was not possible and that the large museum shop sold only the most touristy trinkets. There was only one small table devoted to books, and even then, the one guidebook about the museum's extraordinary collection had only the poorest of illustrations and the most rudimentary text.

I was therefore glad to find that the Shung Ye Museum of Formosan Aborigines was located within very easy walking distance and just down and across the street from the National Palace Museum. Also, admission to the museum was free along with the joint ticket to the Palace Museum.

The museum was easily recognized due to its very modern design and the huge white granite totem pole located in the center of its façade measuring 13.2m (43 ft.) in height. I found that the huge column had been carved with an impressive array of aboriginal designs.

Founded in June of 1994, the ethnographic museum's collection was originally based on that of its founder, Safe C.E. Lin. His desire was to share his personal collection, acquired during many years of collecting, with the public and to further the understanding and appreciation of Taiwan's rich indigenous cultures.

Even today, fourteen indigenous tribes are recognized as living in Taiwan, mostly in the mountainous eastern and southern regions of the island. They have been identified as belonging to Austronesian peoples scattered across Oceania and extending as far west as Madagascar.

Using the latest in exhibition techniques, the museum displays covered a broad spectrum of Formosan indigenous life. Artifacts displayed included pottery, woodcarvings, musical instruments, basketry and ethnic costumes. Also included were objects used in daily life, objects of personal decoration and dress, and ritual artifacts.

In addition to the permanent displays on the ground floor and lower level, there is a gallery for special temporary exhibitions on the basement floor. There is also an auditorium where films and multi-media displays are shown.

With so much of today's Taiwan having been taken over by the Nationalist Chinese escaping from the Communist takeover of mainland China, it is gratifying to see that efforts are being made to preserve and to foster an appreciation of the aboriginal culture of what was Formosa before it became known as Taiwan and the nationalist Republic of China.

Visiting this museum is very worthwhile if you wish to gain an appreciation of modern Taiwan's rich, original, indigenous culture.

Adapted from:

https://en.wikipedia.org/wiki/
Shung_Ye_Museum_of_Formosan_Aborigines
http://www.museum.org.tw/symm_en/01.htm
https://www.tripadvisor.com/Attraction_Review-g293913-d456226-Reviews-
Shung_Ye_Museum_of_Formosan_Aborigines-Taipei.html
https://guidetotaipei.com/visit/shung-ye-museum-of-formosan-aborigines

THAILAND

Country name: Kingdom of Thailand
(formerly Siam)

Site name: Wat Traimit (Temple of the Golden Buddha)

Location: Near the Hualampong Railway Station,
Chinatown District, Bangkok

Date of Visit : 24 December 2005

World's Largest Golden Buddha:
Wat Traimit, Bangkok

Officially named Phra Phuttha Maha Suwan Patimakon, the monumental golden Buddha image today sits in a new, four-story, white marble temple with the official name of Wat Traimit Withayaram Worawihan dedicated on 14 February 2010 and built especially to house its golden image.

For an image of 16 carat gold, the dimensions of the image are especially impressive. It has been measured as being 3m (9.8 ft.) tall and as 3.91m high including its base. From knee to knee, the image has been measured as 3.10m in width.

97

The value of the monumental, golden image is also astounding, estimated at 250 million USD. The image's body has been identified as being 40% pure gold; its face as 80% pure, and its hair and topknot as 99% pure.

Although the origins of the image are not clear, stylistically it had been dated from the 13th-14th centuries and as having been created during the Sukothai period. Due to strong Indian influence during the period, there has been some speculation that parts of the figure may have been made in India. It has been discovered that, to facilitate its being moved, the figure can be separated into nine separate parts and can then be locked together by a key.

The pose of the Buddha is that of *bhumisparsha mudra*, with the right hand touching the earth, symbolizing the enlightenment of Shakyamuni Buddha at Bodh Gaya and the subjugation of Mara. The flame that sits atop the *ushnisha* or topknot of the image is a particularly Sukhothai stylistic feature and symbolizes the deities' spiritual energy. Also typical of such images of the Buddha are the eyebrows that nearly meet in the center, the wrinkles in the neck, the elongated ear lobes and the wide shoulders.

The history of the image and the story of its survival are especially remarkable. An inscription on the so-called Ram Khamhaeng stele is thought to refer to the figure as residing at Sukothai. Then it is thought to have been moved to Ayutthaya from Sukothai sometime around 1403. Probably while at Ayutthaya, the image was plastered over, painted and decorated with inlaid bits of glass. By hiding the image in such a fashion, the image survived the destruction of Ayutthaya by the Burmese in an invasion in 1767.

After King Rama I established his capital at Bangkok, he commanded that ancient Buddhist images from ruined temples around the country to be transported to Bangkok and be set up in newly constructed temples in his new capital. By the time of Rama III, it is known that the figure had been installed in the main building of Bangkok's Wat Chotanaram. Then in 1935, when that temple had fallen into disrepair and had closed, the image was moved to its present location of Wat Traimat.

Being a very minor temple in Bangkok, Wat Traimit was not sufficiently large to house the figure, so it languished for some twenty years, sitting under a tin roof. Only in 1954 was construction undertaken to build a temple suitable for housing the image. Exactly what happened on 25 May of 1955 is not known. Nevertheless, stories agree that the ropes lifting the image to its new location broke, sending the heavy image crashing to the ground. It was then that plaster chipped off the figure and revealed to the stunned workmen the gleaming, gold image hidden underneath.

Ultimately, all the plaster, paint, etc. was finally removed from the image so that even today, there are exhibits at the temple displaying sections of the plaster once covering the figure. Since the discovery of the golden image was close to the celebration of 2500 years since the *parinirvana* of the Buddha, the Thai press published the finding of the Buddha widely, and many Buddhists believed the discovery of the golden image to be a miracle.

Today, the magnificent image sits in a totally new setting from what I saw back in 2005. It now sits on the fourth floor of a new, stepped pagoda completed in 2010. Located on the second story of the new temple is the Yaowarat Chinatown Heritage Center outlining the history of Bangkok's Chinatown. On the third level is an exhibition relating the origins and history of the golden Buddha.

When I first visited Wat Traimet to see the magnificent gold image, I was the only foreign visitor there. By 2005 when I again visited the temple, it had become a major tourist attraction. I can only surmise that today it is packed with tourists as well as the local people.

Bangkok's Emerald Buddha may be the more famous and more sacred image, but in size and magnificence I still regard Wat Traimit's golden image as being, by far, the more astonishing.

Adapted From:

https://en.wikipedia.org/wiki/Golden_Buddha_(statue)

http://bangkokforvisitors.com/chinatown/wat-traimit/index.php

https://www.renown-travel.com/temples/wat-traimit.html

http://www.iamwannee.com/wat-traimit-the-temple-of-golden-buddha/

TUNISIA

Country name: Tunisian Republic
Site name: Hôtel Sidi Driss, also known as the Star Wars Hotel
Location: Matmata, 5 miles south of Gabès
Date Visited: 16 May 2009

Tunisia's Star Wars Hotel

Originally they were ancient troglodyte dwellings. Then they were transformed into a location for a classic science fiction movie. Now they are a hotel and local tourist attraction.

Today the ancient dwellings are known as the Hôtel Sidi Driss, located in the Berber village of Matmata, located 25 miles south of the oasis town of Gabès on the Chott el Jerid.

Matmata is one of Tunisia's best known Berber villages of ancient troglodyte or underground dwellings. It is also one of the largest with approximately 700 of the ancient cave dwellings, some of which are still lived in. Others have become shops, restaurants and hotels. The ancient dwellings were built by first digging large pits into the ground and then by excavating multiple side chambers that are sometimes interconnected by tunnel-like passageways. Excavated from the local rock, the underground dwellings, some hundreds of years old, escape much of the daytime heat by maintaining a year-around temperature of 17 degrees C or 63 degrees F.

While some local residents open their troglodyte homes to tourists, it is the Hôtel Sidi Driss, now often referred to as the Star Wars hotel, that draws the most tourists. In 1976 the ancient dwellings were used as a location for the interior the Lars's homestead on the planet Tatooine in the "Star Wars IV" epic, "A New Hope." It was used as the home of Luke Skywalker as well as that of his Aunt Beru Lars and Uncle Owen Lars. After the Star Wars decor had been removed, the ancient underground dwellings were redecorated and used again as a location in 2000 for the filming of "Star Wars II: Attack of the Clones."

The hotel which is open year around is composed of five underground courtyards, four of them having side rooms. The fifth courtyard with its Star Wars decor still intact functions as the hotel's restaurant.

When the "Star Wars" epics were being made, the hotel's quiet, dimly lit passageways and vaulted rooms were thought to represent the ideal location for the home of the youthful Skywalker on his desert planet of Tatooine.

Today, Matmata has road signs advertising it as a "Star Wars" movie location. Today the residents of Matmata live largely on tourism and on opening their ancient dwellings to visiting tourists.

Adapted from:

https://en.wikipedia.org/wiki/Matmata,_Tunisia
http://wikitravel.org/en/Matmata
http://theswca.com/travel/tunisia/matmata/matmata.html
https://www.greenprophet.com/2013/01/star-wars-tunisia-desert-architecture/

TUNISIA

Country name: Tunisian Republic

Site: North African American Cemetery and Memorial

Maintained by the **American Battle Monuments Commission**

Address: BP 346 Sidi Bou Said, 2026 Tunis, Tunisia

Date Visited: 10 May 2009

An Emotionally Moving Experience: Tunisia's American Military Cemetery

Visiting an American military cemetery located so far removed from the United States was an especially emotionally moving experience.

The North African Cemetery and Memorial is located approximately ten to twelve miles outside of Tunis and five miles from the airport. It is one of twenty-four American cemeteries in foreign countries maintained by the American Battle Monuments Commission (ABMC).

The cemetery was established in 1948 and completed in 1960 and covers 27 acres. Its 2,841 graves of Americans dying in

WWII are arranged in rows divided into nine sections divided by broad walkways. At the intersections of the walkways are ornamental fountains.

In addition to the vast area of the burials, the 364 foot wall of Nahli limestone located along the southeast section of the cemetery, the Wall of the Missing, lists 3,724 names of those missing in action.

At the end of the walkway is the cemetery's chapel and a cloister, the Court of Honor. In the courtyard are walls with colorful mosaics and ceramic panels depicting the WWII operations of the American military across North Africa and into the Persian Gulf.

In the chapel's forecourt stands the Stone of Remembrance of black diorite d'Anzola from Italy. At the stone's base is an inscription adapted from the Bible's Old Testament book of Ecclesiastes. On the cloister's west wall are dedicatory inscriptions in English, French and Arabic.

The cemetery's architects were Moore and Hutchins of New York City. The landscape architect was Bryan J. Lunch, also of New York. Plantings in the cemetery include rows of eucalyptus and ornamental India laurel fig trees as well as many other ornamental shrubs and flower gardens.

In addition to the sounds of the splashing fountains and the sounds of nature, patriotic anthems are played by the chapel's bells from time to time. There are also calls to prayer often heard from nearby mosques.

Since the cemetery actually covers a portion of the ancient city of Carthage, remains of ancient Roman houses and streets can be seen close by. Other remains of ancient Roman Carthage are less than one mile away.

Also, hanging in the cemetery's visitors center, is an ancient Roman floor mosaic originally donated to the American ambassador in 1959 by Tunisia's president Bourguiba and which was later donated to the cemetery.

The cemetery is open to the public Monday through Friday, but is closed on weekends and on American and Tunisian holidays. Staff is usually on duty at the visitors center during visiting hours to assist visitors and to escort them to particular graves or memorial sites.

Visiting the cemetery was, for me, a very harsh reminder of the horrors of war and the terrible toll it takes in human life. But it was gratifying to see that such a magnificent memorial to American service men and women is being so beautifully and carefully maintained on foreign soil. It was also a very educational experience, allowing me to learn much more about the role the military campaign in North Africa during the second World War.

Adapted from:

https://www.abmc.gov/cemeteries-memorials/africa/north-africa-american-cemetery#.WdPGV0vpUnF

http://en.wikipedia.org/wiki/North_Africa_American_Cemetery_and_Memorial

http://www.huffingtonpost.com/magda-abufadil/american-cemetery-in-tunisia_b_1270208.html

http://www.homeofheroes.com/gravesites/abmc/cemeteries/north_africa.html

TURKEY

Country name: Republic of Turkey

Site name: Sultanhani

Location: On the Konya-Aksaray Highway

Date of Visit : 11 November 2011

Sultanhani: Ancient Anatolian Accommodations

It has been called Turkey's largest caravanserai and an outstanding example of Seljuk architecture.

If you were a traveler in 13th century Anatolia, you probably would have thought of it as being luxurious overnight accommodations. You wouldn't have had your choice of a nearby Holiday Inn or a Hilton to check into for a restful night of sleep. Your best bet would have been to find the nearest caravanserai.

Sultanhani (with *hani* meaning caravanserai) is located on the Konya-Aksaray highway and 42 km (26 miles) west of Aksaray and 110 km (68 miles) west of Konya. It is the largest and finest of three large caravanserais in the area. Built along the trade route from Konya to Aksaray that led eventually to Persia, it would probably have been the finest accommodations you'd find in all of Anatolia.

An inscription dates the caravanserai's construction to 1229 CE and during the reign of the Seljuk sultan, Aladdin Kayqubad I. The inscription also names the architect, Muhammad ibn Khahwan al-Dimashqu, with "al-Dimashqi" indicating that he came from Damascus in today's Syria.

After a fire, the caravanserai was restored and extended in 1278 by the local governor, Seraceddin Ahmed Kerimeddin bin el-Hasan. It was after this restoration and extension that Sultanhani became Turkey's largest caravanserai. Since then, the structure has undergone numerous restorations and repairs, the most recent having been completed in the 20th century.

On the exterior, the huge structure gives the appearance of a fortress. Overall, it measures 4,800 square meters. One first enters through a monumental, projecting gateway or *pishtaq* in the eastern wall. The gateway is heavily ornamented with an overhead pointed arch decorated with corbels filled with *muqarnas*, inscriptions and geometric patterns. The eastern front with the watch-towers on its corners measures an impressive 50m in width.

Inside, one finds an open courtyard measuring 44x58m. Along the sides are covered sections or *iwans* that would have been used for storage of goods and for sleeping during warm weather. Located in the center of the courtyard is a small, kiosk-like mosque or *mescit* sitting on four barrel vaults. In its second story is the small mosque itself that can be accessed by large, twin stairways on the structure's west side.

Around the open courtyard surrounded by arcades are stables and covered halls for the storage of goods. In the covered areas are also a kitchen, dining rooms, latrine, repair shops, a Turkish bath, a treasury, and living and sleeping quarters.

At the far end of the courtyard, one finds another monumental entrance decorated with a niche decorated with *muqarnas* and elegant geometric patterns. It leads to a barrel-vaulted central hall with a central nave and side aisles. Four rows of columns, each composed of eight columns, and an array of arches support the barrel vaults as well as the dome in the center in the nave. An oculus in the dome helps to light the dim interior. It is this covered area that would have been used for housing travelers during cooler weather.

Recently, a small village, also named Sultanhani, with shops and businesses providing essential services has grown up surrounding the immense caravanserai.

Entering the Sultanhani was much like entering another much older and much more exotic world than my own. I could imagine that I wouldn't find freshly laundered bed linens, turned down bed covers and a mint sitting on my pillow. Instead, visiting Sultanhani was a revelation of what must have been the life of a Medieval traveler.

Being privileged to see such a magnificent, ancient caravanserai as well as such an outstanding example of Seljuk architecture was one of many highlights of the trip to central Anatolia.

Adapted from:

https://en.wikipedia.org/wiki/Sultan_Han

http://en.wikipedia.org/wiki/Aksaray

http://www.tourmakerturkey.com/sultan-hani-caravanserai.htm

http://www.turkeytravelplanner.com/go/CentralAnatolia/sultanhani/index.html

UZBEKISTAN

Country name: Republic of Uzbekistan

Site name: Ak-Saray

Location: Shakhrisabz, Qashqadaryo region of southern Uzbekistan

UNESCO World Heritage Site: #885, Inscribed 2000

Date of Visit: 10 October 2013

Timur's Immense Summer Palace

Most visitors to Uzbekistan will visit Samarkand and will see the famous Gur Emir, the tomb of Timur the Lame, best known in the West as Tamerlane.

But unless they visit the city of Shakhrisabz, 80 km to the south, they will not see the remains of what was undoubtedly Tamerlane's most grandiose architectural project, the so-called Ak-Saray.

Timur is probably Central Asia's best known ruler. Born on April 9, 1336 in Shakhrisabz, he considered the city his home town and originally planned to have his tomb built there until

109

Samarkand became the larger and more important city, leaving Shakhrisabz somewhat of a backwater town.

Shakhrisabz, meaning "Green City" and known as Kesh in Tamerlane's day, has a number of historic sites worthy of visiting, but the ruins of Timur's summer palace are the primary attraction. Known as the Ak-Saray, meaning "white palace," the huge palace's construction was started in 1380 and lasted twenty-four years. Records show that the palace was constructed by architects and craftsmen from Khwarezm, an area recently conquered by Timur. An inscription gives the date of the completion of the palace as 798 AH (1395-6 CE), but completing the decoration of the palace probably took much longer. Another inscription gives the name of Muhammad Yusuf Tebrizi from the city of Tabriz as one of the craftsmen working on the palace.

Unfortunately, all that remains of the grandiose palace are the enormous pylons of a *pishtaq*, the projecting elements of an *iwan* or a large, formal gateway. It is estimated that the portal must have originally stood at a height of 70 meters. Topped by arched pinnacles it had corner towers some 80 meters high set on multifaceted pedestals. The immense entryway is thought to have measured 50 meters in width, while its archway is thought to have been Central Asia's largest, spanning 22.5 meters.

Fortunately, a Spanish ambassador, Ruy Gonzalez de Clavijo, visited Shakhrisabz in 1404 and left a detailed description of the magnificent palace. He described it as having a large courtyard around which many living and service quarters were grouped. The main courtyard is estimated to have measured 120-124 meters wide and 240-250 meters long. He also described the palace as having meadows and shady gardens filled with fruit trees and formal pools. Today, climbing the 116 steps to the top of the surviving ruins not only provides visitors with views of the surrounding countryside but will give them more of an appreciation of the original immensity of the palace's size.

Tradition credits Abdullakhan as having destroyed the immense palace and killing Timur's descendants in his sieges to conquer Shahrisabz. By the 18th century only the pillars and the arch of the palace's primary entrance remained.

Today, the palace ruins have been largely left free of the often dubious Russian reconstructions and restorations seen elsewhere in Central Asia. Even as fragments, one cannot help but be impressed by the refinement of the tile designs and the sophistication of the colors of blue, white and gold, glazed decoration. In addition to the complex geometric ornament and exquisite foliate designs are inscriptions from the Koran.

Today, a modern statue of Timur stands at a distance from the surviving ruins of the palace portal in what was once the huge palace's central courtyard. The day of our visit, the statue was the crowded scene of wedding parties taking photographs.

Even in its highly ruinous state, the Ak-Saray can't help but impress with its extraordinary scale, its exceptionally refined ornament and the grandeur of Timur's architectural conception.

A side trip from Samarkand to Shakhrisabz, one of Uzbekistan's five UNESCO World Heritage Sites, and visiting the ruins of the Ak-Saray is strongly recommended when visiting Central Asia's five "Stans."

Adapted from:
https://en.wikipedia.org/wiki/Shahrisabz
http://whc.unesco.org/en/list/885
http://www.advantour.com/uzbekistan/shakhrisabz/ak_saray.htm

VIETNAM

Country name: Socialist Republic of Vietnam

Site name: Museum of Cham Sculpture

Location: In the Hai Chau District, near the Han River, Danang, Vietnam

Tour Dates: 4-17 December 2009

Vietnam's Lost Kingdom:
Museum of Cham Sculpture, Danang

The visit to Vietnam's archaeological site of My Son was heartbreaking. I had visited My Son the day before our visit to the Museum of Cham Sculpture in Danang.

My Son is located 40 km southwest of Hoi An, and we had arrived at a hotel very near the ancient site. We had a half day at leisure, and fortunately, our local guide found a driver that would take me out to visit My Son. None of the other tour members were interested in visiting the site designated a UNESCO World Heritage Site (no. 949) in 1999.

My Son is said to have been the longest inhabited archaeological site in Indochina. Considered the most important intellectual and religious center of the Cham kingdom, My Son flourished from the 2nd to 15th centuries. Most of the Cham temples there were dedicated to the Hindu deity, Shiva, regarded as the protector of the Champa dynasties.

Little did I realize that most of what I would find at My Son would be ruins. Of the seventy structures discovered there by French archaeologists in the late 1890s, only twenty have escaped irreparable damage. Especially during and after the Tet Offensive in 1968, massive bombing raids by the U.S. resulted in widespread destruction at My Son. It is thought that most of My Son was bombed into oblivion in U.S. bombing in a single week during the Vietnam War.

Even today, much of the area remains mined. Grazing cattle are killed, and Vietnamese are still being maimed and killed by the unexploded ordnance. Visitors to the site are warned to stay on marked paths. Today, archaeologists, with the aid of UNESCO, are now struggling to piece together what little remains of My Son, but much has been lost forever.

I was therefore encouraged when we visited the Museum of Cham Sculpture in Danang. I found that much has been preserved in the museum from the Kingdom of Cham that ruled southern Vietnam from 192 to 1697 CE. The museum houses the world's largest collection of Cham sculpture and is reputed to contain nearly three hundred stone and terra cotta sculptures dating from the 7th to 15th centuries.

The only museum of its kind in the world, it was first named the Henry Parmenties Museum, after the name of its founder whose collection had initially formed the basis for the museum. Originally many of the works of art had been exhibited in a sculpture garden called "Le Jardin de Tourrane" on a low hill near the Han River in Danang. Designed by French architects, M. Deleval and M. Auclair, the present museum building sits on the same site. Founded in 1915 by the École Française d'Extrême

Orient (EFEO), the museum is now housed in a building designed to reflect both Western and Cham elements.

The original museum building has been enlarged twice. The first expansion was in the 1930s when two galleries were added to house works of art collected in the 1920s and 1930s. In 2002 the second expansion of the museum took place, providing an additional thousand square meters of space, so now the two-story building houses not only galleries but spaces for museum staff, a restoration shop, library and storage. Some pieces of sculpture are also exhibited outdoors in the forecourt of the museum building.

Today the museum contains ten galleries, each devoted to the site where the works of art were originally discovered. In addition to a gallery containing sculptures from My Son, there are those containing works from the archaeological sites of Kon Tum, Binh Dinh, Quang Tri, Quang Ngai, Thap Mam, Tra Kieu and Dong Duong. Signs have been installed inside each gallery just inside the entrances to the various rooms giving information in Vietnamese, French and English. Guidebooks in English are also available.

Most of the sculptures in the museum are temple altars, Hindu images, and fragments of architectural decoration. Since most Champa architecture is of brick, sculptors carved objects separately that would then be incorporated into the architecture.

In large part unknown to the outside world, the Kingdom of Champa ruled large sections of central Vietnam for eight centuries. With its golden age from the 7th to 10th centuries, the kingdom ruled an area extending from south of the Ngang Pass to the delta of the Dong Nai River. Strongly influenced by early Hinduism, it is thought that the kingdom extended its influence to control much of the trade between China, India and the Indonesian islands.

Prior to my visit of Vietnam, I had known almost nothing about the culture of Champa or about Cham art, so both my visits to My Son and to the museum in Danang were revelations about an aspect of Asian art that is so little known and appreciated. It also demonstrated to me what little regard we often have for other cultures and how easily we can wantonly destroy the magnificent monuments of their ancient culture.

Adapted from:

https://en.wikipedia.org/wiki/Museum_of_Cham_Sculpture

http://www.vietnam-guide.com/da-nang/cham-museum.htm

http://www.vietnam-beauty.com/cities/da-nang/6-da-nang/277-the-cham-museum.html

https://www.travelfish.org/sight_profile/vietnam/central_vietnam/da_nang/da_nang/405

https://www.victoriahotels.asia/blog/visiting-the-spectacular-cham-sculpture-museum-in-danang/

http://whc.unesco.org/en/list/949

https://en.wikipedia.org/wiki/Mỹ_Sơn

VIETNAM

Country Name: Socialist Republic of Vietnam

Subject: Water Puppet Shows

Location: Outdoor performance seen at the Museum of
Ethnology (Bao Tang Don Toc Hoc), Hanoi

Indoor performance seen at the Thang Long Water Puppet
Theater, Hanoi, Address: 57B, Dinh Tien Hoang Street, Hoan
Kiem District, Hanoi

Tour Dates: 4-17 December 2009

Vietnam's Unique Water Puppet Shows

Puppet shows seen while on various trips to Southeast Asia
have been among my most memorable experiences. Before
visiting Vietnam, I had seen marionette shows in Myanmar and
a shadow puppet play in Yogyakarta, Java.

But the most unique puppet performances seen in Southeast
Asia were the water puppet shows seen in Hanoi, Vietnam. The
first such show was seen indoors at the Thang Long Water
Puppet Theater in Hanoi. Although enjoyable, the show was
held in a dimly lighted theater and was not conducive to
photography. It was also obviously staged for tourists.

The second show was seen by chance in an outdoor pond while visiting Hanoi's Museum of Ethnology. Puppeteers were hidden behind an elaborate stage set up at the one end of the pond while musicians played and soloists sang traditional songs at one side. The show was being watched primarily by the local Vietnamese people who ringed the pond seated on low benches, with only a very few tourists such as myself.

The Vietnamese water puppet show tradition dates back to the 11th century CE and originated in the Red River area in northern Vietnam. The puppeteers stand waist deep in water tanks behind a hanging screen and manipulate the puppets attached to long rods hidden beneath the water's surface. A series of pulleys and cords give action to the many carved and lacquered, wooden figures.

Performances are accompanied by an orchestra playing traditional music using drums, wooden bells, horns, bamboo flutes and cymbals. Vietnamese operatic songs are sung telling the story that is being acted out by the puppets. The shows usually tell folk tales and legends with one popular subject being the celebration of the rice harvest.

Performances often include a number of short skits and take the audience on a journey through ancient village life, agricultural harvests and dances of mythical creatures. The stories often have a humorous element, and the live music plays an important part of the show with singers sometimes shouting encouragement to the puppets.

The traditional Vietnamese music performed throughout the shows enhances the action of the puppets, rising to crescendos of sound at the most dramatic moments in the stories. Special effects can also be used creating fire-breathing dragons, smoke-filled battles and celebrations complete with fireworks. Especially popular are the often violent fights between brightly painted river monsters.

Today, performances may be given in traditional village ponds where a stage has been set up, on portable tanks for traveling performances, or in special theaters where a stage containing a pool has been constructed.

One of the most popular water puppet characters is Chu Teu. *Chu* means "uncle, man, or boy" while *teu* means "laugh" in Vietnamese. He acts as a jester and provides witty comments on Vietnamese political and social life. He appears as a smiling boy, often wearing only a loincloth and open vest.

At the end of the performances, the screen hiding the puppeteers is lifted or they emerge from behind the screen at the backs of the tanks to receive the applause of the audience.

I found the water puppet plays among the most enjoyable, authentic, and unique aspects of Vietnamese culture witnessed on my trip.

I even felt compelled to purchase a copy of a jolly little water puppet with his large, grinning face at one of Hanoi's touristy shops as a souvenir of the trip.

Adapted from:

https://en.wikipedia.org/wiki/Water_puppetry

www.thanglongwaterpuppet.org

http://www.vietnam-guide.com/hanoi/water-puppet-theatre.htm

Appendix I
A Dummy's Guide to Travel Photography

This is a dummy's guide to travel photography. It is advice coming from someone who is admittedly very much an amateur travel photographer. It offers very few guidelines on the technical aspects of photography. It is a guide primarily for amateur photographers such as myself and not for those who are professionals and are technically proficient. There will be no discussions of various types of cameras, ISOs, various digital photography file formats, etc.

It is estimated that 880 billion photographs are taken each year and that some 1.8 billion are added to the internet every day. Such staggering figures make a photographer such as myself wonder if he should be taking any photographs at all, only to add to the enormous gut of visual images already in the world.

Especially if you are an amateur travel photographer, how can you create images that convey your impressions and concerns about the countries you have visited and make impactful photographs that adequately reflect your experiences as a traveler?

Nevertheless, I've found that photographs help to keep alive my memories of a particular trip and provide a visual record of my trips abroad as nothing else has been able to do.

When I first began traveling, I decided not to take photographs but to purchase guidebooks, brochures, etc. about the places I'd visited. The photos in the guidebooks would be far better than any I might take myself, or so I thought.

I soon found my bookshelves cluttered with many small travel guides that I never actually found the time to look at. The photos also had an impersonal look to them, and they didn't reflect my personal experiences while on a trip but only those of professional photographers.

So it was during my first trip after retiring that I took with me to Egypt a brand new, small, digital camera and became a traveler intent on taking photographs reflecting my own, very personal travel experiences.

As an amateur photographer, I take with me only point-and-shoot, digital cameras on a trip. I take two cameras with the second one as a backup. I also take several spare memory cards, several rechargeable batteries and the equipment for recharging them. I also take a collection of electrical outlet converters for the various electrical wall outlets found abroad in accommodations when traveling.

Rather than lugging around expensive and elaborate photographic equipment, I much prefer being inconspicuous and blending into the local scene as much as possible. I prefer traveling light, enabling me to be much more mobile and flexible. It often allows me to carry everything with me on airplanes and to avoid the checked baggage fees. It also bypasses the often long waits at the carousels in the baggage claim areas, since my luggage is already with me.

Does better photographic equipment make for better photographs? I say: not necessarily. One instructor in a photography course I took once said that a photograph winning him a major prize was of children on a playground taken with a Brownie camera. Another of my photography instructors had all the professional bells and whistles in his elaborate array of photographic equipment. Somehow, the second instructor's photographs never impressed me all that much. The first instructor, a certified Abode Photoshop trainer, had photos that I thought had better compositions and more interesting subject matter.

Many of the general rules and recommendations of professional photographers also apply to travel photography. Some of the more common ones are as follows.

Use the rules of composition to your advantage. Use the rule of thirds, separating your photo's composition into three areas both horizontally and vertically. Then place prominent elements in the photo on those lines. As an example, position the statue on one of the lines rather than right in the photo's center.

Give your photo a point of interest. A photograph of a panoramic landscape can look flat and uninteresting. Try adding something such as a section of a highway curving off in the distance or a small building. Adding a tree or bush to one side can give a landscape a depth it might not have otherwise.

Use leading lines and diagonals. A view of a long street filled with people can add diagonal lines and spice up a city view. Try photographing buildings on the diagonal rather than head on.

Focus closely in on your subject rather than using only general views. Try taking detail views of buildings, highlighting a piece of architectural decoration. Take detail views of pieces of sculpture and monuments. Your photos may look more unique and interesting when using more unusual views.

Avoid distracting elements. Change your vantage point to cut out the view of the trash rotting in the corner of a building. Try to exclude electrical and telephone wires. A view of a beautiful sky can be ruined by strands of electrical wires. The spectacular façade of a cathedral might be bisected by a thick, black electrical cable. Such things can often be painted out during the post-trip processing of photographs, but the process can be tricky and tedious.

Include people. This is a rule I should use more often. I often exclude people to focus on the cityscape or the architecture rather than on people. Why include tour group members or people in Western attire when they say nothing about the exotic location you're visiting? On the other hand, when in India, I always attempt to include women in their saris whenever possible. I feel that they add much to the exoticism of the sites I've visited in India. The priests and religious elders in their regalia and carrying their ceremonial umbrellas added much to the photographs taken when witnessing the Ethiopian Christians' celebration of Timket.

Including people can also often be used to good effect to convey a sense of scale. A group of people photographed in front the façade of a cathedral can give a greater sense of the building's monumental size.

In many more touristy locations, there are those there primarily to be photographed. Street performers can make for great photographs as can street vendors showing off their wares. A small tip might be required but may be well worth it if it you can get an outstanding photograph.

Try to capture candid rather than posed photographs of people. I took a view of a Tibetan nun in Shimla, India, who was very intent on turning a series of prayer wheels. When she turned and smiled at the camera, the second photograph I took of her seemed much less interesting.

Unfortunately, there are those other photographers who feel they have every right to stand in front of whatever you're waiting to photograph to take selfies or to have their friends photograph them. One after another they stand with ginning faces posing for one photograph after another. Others parade around with selfie sticks taking multiple photographs of themselves. Do they realize how much they appear to be in love with themselves?

I try not to be invasive when photographing people. It can be viewed as an invasion of their personal privacy. I try shooting the backs of people walking down a village street or photographing only people at a distance if they are facing my camera.

Avoid photographing policemen, security guards, soldiers, etc. unless it's obvious that they are there to be photographed. When in doubt, it is best first to ask or use sign language to get their permission.

What may be photographed in a foreign country and what may not may become become a serious problem when traveling. It's best to be overly cautious and to consult with a local guide as to what must not be photographed. Be especially cautious if you are sightseeing on your own.

Avoid photographing government buildings, embassies, prisons, etc. As an example, guards rushed out to ban my photographing the American embassy in Phnom Penh, Cambodia.

An especially ugly incident occurred in Ashgabat, the capital of the police state of Turkmenistan. While photographing city views on my own, I inadvertently took a photograph of the country's presidential palace. I was immediately accosted by two policemen. They demanded that I hand over my camera and proceeded to delete all the photographs I'd taken from the camera's memory card. Fortunately half of the photographs from the trip to Central Asia were not lost forever. After my return, I found a local photo service that could retrieve all the deleted photographs.

Later, I learned that the secret to keeping such deleted photographs is not to take any more photographs on the same memory card. Taking new photographs may permanently override and destroy the older ones. So if you think your photographs may be lost forever, you may find a local photo service which can retrieve them for you.

The presidential palace, Ashgabat, Turkmenistan
Note the two policemen at the lower right coming to delete
the photographs from my camera's memory card.

Avoid using the digital zoom on your camera. It will only enlarge the number of pixels in a digital image. Optical zoom is preferable. Better yet, try moving in toward what you're photographing.

Which is better, vertical or horizontal photographs? I usually use the scene itself to be the guide. Which fits best inside the frame of your photograph? On the other hand, horizontal photographs always seem to look better on computers and TV screens.

Avoid taking photographs out of car or bus windows. Even if it's only a very short photo stop, it's best to get out and explore the area for photo opportunities. You may very well discover something serendipitously that you'd otherwise have missed. You may also often find better vantage points. If there is no stop, attempt to take a photograph when the car or bus has stopped, such as at a traffic signal. If taking a photograph while the vehicle is in motion, avoid photographing nearby objects as they are likely to appear blurred. One of my best photographs was taken from a tour bus window while on the trip to Cuba. Our stops at historic sites were so few and far between, that often there was no alternative but to photograph from behind a window.

Especially when traveling, serendipity can often result in your taking some of your best trip photographs. Attempt to train yourself to search for photo opportunities and to look around and behind you for things to be photographed that you may not initially be aware of. The temple sitting beside the small lake that you spot just before you board the tour bus may provide you with one of your best photographs from a trip. Having a trained eye can often separate the photographer with the outstanding photos from the photographer with only mediocre photographs.

There are two widely divergent schools of thought about processing photographs after returning from a trip. The first is that you should shoot the best possible photograph and leave it entirely alone. The second is that you'll do your best to improve your photographs by processing them after your trip. I'm of the second school. I try to bring out detail in areas in shadow. I crop photos to eliminate distracting elements. I correct the color. I eliminate lens distortions and sharpen the image as much as possible. My goal is to create the best possible photograph without falsifying the image. As a result, I've even received comments such as, "how did you get those photos out of that tiny, little camera?"

For storing the thousands of photographs taken during fourteen years of travel, I burn my own computer discs on my personal computer. I buy blank DVDs rather than CDs, since the DVDs allow for more digital storage space. In order to retain a higher resolution, I save photographs as 5x7.5 inch images with 300 dpi (dots per inch) resolution and save the files as JPEGs in the RGB mode. Then when making photo prints, I convert the files to the more standard 4x6 inch size and find that I can digitally send my JPEG photo files to a local photographic service. Then I can usually pick up the photo prints the next day.

Rather than storing photo prints in bulky albums, I maintain a bookcase shelf of photo discs in plastic jewel cases only about a foot in length. Located next to my computer work area, I can easily reach over, select the disc I want, pop the disc into my compact disc reader, find the folder on the disc, and then locate the photo I want. I've found that such a system makes the thousands of travel photos I've taken easily accessible.

Finding a use for all the thousands of travel photographs I've taken has been a much larger problem. The primary purpose for storing the photographs has always been to preserve them for my own personal use. They have served as a most valuable visual record of my various trips. They have done much to keep the memories of my trips alive. They have also often spurred me on to search for more information on many of the sites I've visited. They have done much to broaden my knowledge and interests in other parts of the world.

The photographs have also become very useful when giving programs at a local travel group. It has been possible to create animated slide shows shown on a TV screen located in a private meeting room of a local restaurant where the travel group meets monthly

I've also used the travel photographs in experiments such as pasting a series of photographs together to form long panoramas. I've experimented when making covers for the plastic jewel cases in which I store the computer discs. I've modified photos with various filters and special effects in PhotoShop which I've then been downloaded to the website, deviantart,com. Selections of the travel photos have also been downloaded on the website, flickr.com.

Making photo books has been much less successful. Several photo books were made on blurb.com. They were expensive, and there was little market for them. Shutterfly.com has been used to make DVDs with slide shows, but there has always been a significant loss of resolution in the photos. Again, I found no market for the DVDs.

Even after many years as a travel photographer, I've found that there is always still much more to be learned. I need to capture more of a sense of place in the photographs. More attention is needed on what the photographs should be communicating to the observer. More is needed to capture the excitement I've felt when visiting many of the sites visited on a trip. The photos often don't have the aesthetic appeal and the humanistic, documentary qualities I wish they might have. I have found that, as with almost all aspects of human endeavor, one can only attempt to grow and develop in such a chosen field.

Traveling as a photographer has led me down paths I never would have otherwise imagined possible. I have developed a wanderlust, an almost insatiable addiction to travel. It has given me a passion and desire to explore strange new worlds and new cultures and to go boldly where I've not gone before.

Appendix II
A Dummy's Guide to Photography in Museums

Taking photographs while on a trip seems difficult enough, but circumventing all the byzantine rules and regulations set up by many foreign museums often creates even more hassles for the traveling photographer.

This is therefore advice from an amateur travel photographer who has taken photographs in museums in many parts of the world. Not being any sort of professional photographer, there will be very few, suggestions including the arcane, technical advice usually found in such articles.

First and foremost, it's best to determine if photography is permitted or banned inside a foreign museum. When entering a museum, try to determine as soon as possible whether or not anything at all can be photographed, either from an English-speaking guide or from someone at an admissions desk.

Especially when traveling abroad, there is often an additional charge for the privilege of photographing inside a museum. Usually the charge is minimal, only up to the equivalent of about $5 USD. You are usually given a special ticket, in addition to the admissions ticket, which should be kept with you throughout your museum visit, indicating you've paid for photography privileges to show museum guards if you're asked.

If the charge for photography is significantly more, beware. It's probably not worth it. The cost of photographing inside the glitzy museum building in Ashgabat, Turkmenistan, was close to $18 USD. To my dismay, I found little of interest inside the museum that I felt merited being photographed. Along with many other countries in central Asia that had once been part of the Soviet Union, Turkmenistan had been raped by Soviet archaeologists of most of its major antiquities. Also, I was informed at one point by a museum staff member that I'd wandered off into an area of the museum where photography was not permitted, even after our local guide had encouraged me to visit the museum shop located in what was said to be the restricted area.

Even if you have paid for photographing inside a museum, it is best to ask if there are any special objects or areas in the museum that are restricted. The general rule at most museums is that objects in the museum's permanent collection are fair game for photographing. Be wary of special exhibitions, however, where photographing works of art belonging to other collections might be restricted. Whenever in doubt, ask. Taking videos in museums is another matter altogether. It is often banned, and if permitted at all, usually involves paying an additional and much higher fee for the privilege.

The Savitsky Collection, Nukus, Uzbekistan. A view gotten only because I took my camera with me when visiting the museum.

In one instance, even taking a camera zipped in a camera case created a major problem. At the Savitsky Collection in Nukus, Uzbekistan, my camera and its case were confiscated and locked in a large, steel safe in the museum's cloak room. I was given a large key to the safe along with the stern warning that I must not lose the key. It was the only key they had for the safe. Later, I was berated by our local guide for even bringing the camera into the museum, when I had brought it with me only to take photographs outside the museum. Would I have been allowed the time to retrieve my camera from the tour bus to take photographs outside the museum? Of course not.

Even if photography inside a museum is banned, photography of objects displayed in areas outside the museum might be permitted. It is often worthwhile to take views of the exterior of the museum building and of the signage outside the museum. Often on-location signs give information not found elsewhere. Many museum buildings are outstanding works of architecture in their own right and function as good subjects for photographs. In addition to general views, there are often pieces of sculpture and architectural decoration that make for good subjects to photograph. Inside, museum lobbies, signs, museum ground plans, and gallery installation views also might make for worthwhile photographs.

When visiting foreign museums, looking very much like an amateur photographer usually pays off. It's best to remain inconspicuous and as someone very intent on following all the museum's rules, regardless of how unreasonable they may appear. I recommend bringing only a point-and-shoot camera, a spare memory card and spare batteries. Museum officials often become very wary of those coming in, lugging large, professional cameras and sizable bags of camera equipment. Especially if you're tempted to bring in tripods or monopods, just don't.

If questioned as to why you want to photograph inside a museum, it's best to say that your photographs are for your private use or for non-commercial, educational purposes. Even if I use a photograph in an article I've written for such a publication as *International Travel News (ITN)*, I can say it has been used for non-commercial purposes since writers for *ITN* are not monetarily compensated. If you use any photographs of a museum object in a publication you might later make available for sale, be especially careful of infringing on copyrights.

Most museums abroad are usually not crowded except for many of the major museums in Europe. Problems with museum visitors inhibiting taking photographs inside a museum usually come from large groups of the local people, school groups and especially members of your own tour group. In many museums abroad, our tour group usually had the museums all to ourselves.

The National Palace Museum in Taipei, Taiwan, was an exception. It was so crowded with local people and school groups that it soon became became one of the least satisfactory museum tours I've ever experienced anywhere, including many of the overly crowded museums in New York City.

The gargantuan National Palace Museum, Taipei, Taiwan

Also, especially troublesome are those in museums that must take numerous selfies of themselves in front of every object that you would also like to photograph. They pose in front of objects and endlessly trade off taking photographs of each other. They must also take endless views of an object.

130

Meanwhile, while you are waiting, your tour group has disappeared. The only alternative is usually to practice infinite patience. Wait until you get a clear view of what you want to photograph, quickly take your photograph, and then rush to rejoin your group.

Museum lighting can become another serious problem. Often it's very dim and deliberately so to protect objects that are light sensitive. If tempted to use flash, don't. The very intense flashes of light may cause irreparable damage to works of art and archaeological objects. Using flash photography may not only incur the wrath of museum guards but will usually create washed out areas in your photographs as well as areas in unnatural, dark shadow. When in museums, permanently set the flash off on your camera.

Museum lighting can also create photographs with undesirable color casts, often a sickly yellow. Although camera filters might help, it's best to leave such camera accessories outside. Post-trip processing of photographs can often correct such color changes in a version of PhotoShop. Museums also often have a tendency to use lighting for dramatic effects by spotlighting objects in their displays. Try to find the best view of the object and hope for the best when processing your photographs later.

Museum showcases are another bane of the photographer. Glass always seems to reflect light in exactly those areas where the objects you're attempting to photograph are located. Try different vantage points so the reflections appear in areas that can be cropped or painted out later. If the object is in a display case, it's often best not even to attempt to photograph it and to concentrate on objects in a gallery that are not exhibited behind glass.

Reflections from varnished paintings are another bane of the photographer. Again, try different vantage points. Sometimes reflections disappear if your vantage point is to one side of the painting. Distortions in the dimensions of paintings in photographs can then be rectified later by post-trip photo processing. Sometimes, taking only a detail view of an object rather than photographing the entire object itself can circumvent getting such reflections.

When photographing paintings, prints, etc., the question often becomes whether or not to include the frame. If the frame is an integral part of the work or art or an especially interesting one, I may include it in the photograph. If I do, I usually take another photo of the object without the frame. For the most part, I refrain from photographing frames since I'd rather that the focus be on the work of art itself than its frame.

Sculpture and other three-dimensional objects present their own special problems. I recommend that you attempt to establish what you feel is its most characteristic view. Which view shows the object off to the best advantage? Three-dimensional objects often lend themselves to taking numerous photographs. Later, a decision can be made as to which view is the best. If an object is displayed against a wall or a similar background, it's usually to your advantage when attempting to avoid distracting details. If the object is displayed in the center of a museum gallery, finding a view that has the fewest background distractions can become a serious problem.

Many photographers will photograph museum objects, only to realize later that they have little or no information about what they have photographed. Labels next to objects and other signage in museum galleries often give information you'll not find elsewhere. Why not take a photograph just for the documentation they provide?

Image stabilization can also become a problem in museums. There are those who advise propping yourself up next to walls, doorways, showcases, etc. They also propose placing your camera directly on the glass of display cases. I strongly advise against it, unless you want an encounter with museum guards. I recommend placing your feet apart, holding your arms tightly to your sides, and holding your breath when taking a photo. If you think you've inadvertently moved when taking a photo, take another.

When all else fails, when the photographs you've taken turn out badly, and when you can't even photograph inside a museum, there are other solutions, of sorts. Visit the museum shop or ask if there are any museum catalogs or other publications available for sale. Even if in a foreign language, such publications often have good photographs of objects in museum collections. Once back in the States, you can scan in the photographs. After the disastrous visit at the National Palace Museum in Taiwan, I consulted the Amazon website and located a very large, scholarly catalog of the museum's collection at a very reasonable price. The shop in the museum in Taipei had only one table for books and only a very mediocre, small book about the museum's collection. At least I now have an appropriate souvenir of having visited the museum, one reputed to be the world's finest and largest collections of Chinese art.

Another last resort is the internet where you'll find photographs that, to use a euphemism, can be appropriated. If you add such photographs from the internet as well as photos you've scanned in from catalogs to those you've actually taken yourself, it should be essential that you add a credit line somewhere on the photo about the source of the photo. Such credit lines can be added in small type to a bottom corner of a photograph using a version of PhotoShop.

If you don't attempt photographing in foreign museums, it is my belief that you will not have the most comprehensive visual documentation of your trip, one of the primary reasons for taking your travel photographs in the first place.

Made in the USA
Lexington, KY
18 November 2017